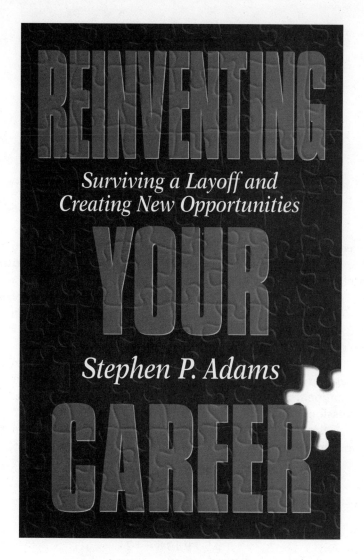

REINVENTING

*Surviving a Layoff and
Creating New Opportunities*

YOUR

Stephen P. Adams

CAREER

NORTHFIELD PUBLISHING
CHICAGO

ISBN: 1-881273-61-X

1 3 5 7 9 10 8 6 4 2

Printed in the United States of America

To my wife, Mary Jane

CONTENTS

PREFACE

A sign on the wall at the Cuyahoga County Reemployment Services Center in Cleveland, Ohio, may not be the most appetizing message for a lunchroom, but it gets to the point:

"If you have to swallow a toad, don't spend too much time looking at it."

To the jobless people who pass through these halls, the message connects. Losing a job can be like staring eyeball to eyeball with a fat, ugly toad and waiting to see who blinks first. You have two basic choices—let yourself become paralyzed by the unpalatable circumstances or swallow hard and move on.

Often there's a crushing load of discouragement, rejection, self-pity, even shame. Sometimes there's anger and bitterness toward the heartless former employer or a former boss who ought to be wearing a black hat—over his horns. The temptation is to dwell on the past to the exclusion of the future. Counselors encourage the jobless to deal with their circumstances just like a death in the family—allow time for the natural grieving process, then get on with life.

This book is not about pointing fingers. In today's global village and mass media glutted with sensationalism, sex, and violence, there is more than enough blame and scandal to go around. Yes, there is the smell of money in the air and the shadow of greed over the land, but that's not the whole story. Social forces larger than a political campaign platform or a Pulitzer Prize nomination are afoot. They won't go away easily—or soon.

Reinventing Your Career, as the name suggests, is about dealing. It's about getting on with life.

What do you do after the pink slip arrives, when your services are no longer needed or your job no longer exists? Blame and resentment won't pay the rent. Unemployment compensation will only keep food on the table for so long. There comes a point where we have to pick ourselves up and, as the Old Blue Eyes song goes, get back into the race. It may be a rat race, but you don't have to be trapped like one. There is healing, and there are ways to prepare to face a future that only promises to present more of the same.

So, that's easy for me to say? Not really. I've been there.

Of life's stressors—traumatic setbacks, disasters, and catastrophes—most people would list things like the death of a child, death of a spouse, and loss of a job. Within a relatively short period of time, I experienced two of those three. The last thing I would call those experiences is easy.

Nine years and two careers ago, I worked for a newspaper that was experiencing major upheavals in management as one executive toppled another from power, only to be felled in turn by yet another. In the process, a number of people were caught in the crossfire, including me. As an assistant city editor, I was in as high a supervisory position as I could be and remain within union jurisdiction. So I couldn't be fired without cause, but life could be made so miserable that I would want to quit.

And miserable it became. I was demoted, reduced in pay, and assigned to a night shift in a dead-end position that was a real career-killer—the "bonepile," one co-worker called it. But the worst part was family life. It ceased to exist. Every day, my children would come home from school about a half hour after I'd left for work. Every night I would come home to a darkened house where dinner had been eaten, bedtime stories read, and prayers said without Dad.

It was the proverbial slow death by a thousand cuts. For nearly two years I struggled with anger, bitterness, discouragement, and even depression while I searched fruitlessly for another newspaper job in America, hating every morning that the sun rose on another day of frustration. In fact, I never did find another newspaper job. In the process, I struggled with feelings of resentment every time I sensed that being a forty-year-old white male was working against me in my profession.

This first reversal of fortune was a bit ahead of the wave of corporate downsizings that was to make such experiences commonplace in the 1990s. My escape then was through a career change. I took a job in public relations, which actually came with a pay increase. But it meant turning my back on a twenty-year newspaper career, since I would be going over to the other side by becoming a PR "flack."

Six years later, I found out firsthand about the scary new realities of corporate America when two of us at this company were called in on a Monday morning and told our services were no longer needed. I was shocked and numb. The long ride home felt like a kind of death. Breaking the news at home made me feel like a king-sized heel, letting down my family big-time.

But personally I was also oddly relieved, having worked under extremely stressful conditions for some time. Still, I had been receiving regular raises and even a promotion. This was the kind of thing that happened to other people, not to me. I didn't know then that relief is the second stage in the grief process, right after the initial shock.

But it wasn't as if I had a lot of reserves to draw on. Just fifteen months earlier, my wife and I had lost a child— a newborn son, who lived two weeks and then succumbed to complications of Rh disease. We had known the circumstances were difficult, but until the last day, we struggled to believe that we were going to take that child home. We were wrong.

So the job loss was actually the second trauma. Looking back honestly, I can believe that my work performance over those subsequent months may have been less than stellar with my beaten-down frame of mind and burned-out energy level. I certainly wasn't very resilient to stress, which had become a way of life in that period. I may have inadvertently nominated myself to be one of the employees to walk the corporate plank.

But that's not the whole story. In the midst of adversity, some positive things had been happening. Looking back again, I can even say that the two job losses were blessings in disguise, considering some of the things that came out of those experiences. In the pages of *Reinventing Your Career*, we will meet a few other individuals for whom losing a job was not the end of the world but actually the beginning of a new, if not better, life.

In the first three chapters we will look at the roots of the downsizing/layoff phenomenon and what it represents, and then at real case studies of four women and three men whose lives were changed forever by job upheaval. The results may be surprising. There can be worse things than losing a job, and chapter 4 looks at the downside of staying in a bad job in terms of issues like workaholism and codependency. In chapters 5 and 6 we explore the value of discovering a sense of personal purpose and mission in work life and taking inventory of one's skills, talents, and abilities to identify core competencies. We then meet in chapters 7 and 8 the composite character Jerry Davenport, who takes us through the career counseling process for a couple of chapters, dealing with emotional and self-esteem issues and then practical job-search skills and strategies. Chapter 9 is a forward-looking examination of new work/lifestyles, such as telecommuting, self-employment, home-based businesses, and the virtual office. Finally, we consider the ultimate mission—our life purpose—in chapter 10. Helpful resources are listed in the Appendix.

A sign on the wall at the Cuyahoga County Reemployment Services Center quotes Warren Bennis, author and distinguished professor of business administration at the University of Southern California: "The factory of the future will have only two employees, a man and a dog. The man will be there to feed the dog. The dog will be there to keep the man from touching the equipment."

One way or another, most people have been affected by layoffs and downsizing or know somebody who has. And, as we'll see, everyone is affected, not just those who have lost a job. Those who keep their jobs are indirectly involved through something called "layoff survivor syndrome."

I say that my own job losses were blessings in disguise because of the fruit they produced in my life that I wouldn't have experienced any other way. Another sign at the Cuyahoga County Reemployment Services Center, where I attended a job services program, said: "'Mountaintops inspire leaders, but valleys mature them.'—J. Phillip Epperson."

The fact was, I needed maturing. During the death throes of my newspaper career, I was asked to teach an adult Sunday school class on the New Testament book of Philippians. If you're not sure God has a sense of humor, picture a bummed-out, washed-up journalist trying to teach a class on the book of the Bible most concerned with *joy*—not just ignorant bliss, but a heart that rejoices despite adverse people, things, and circumstances. Let's just say that the teacher had to learn about the magic of enthusiasm—a lesson well learned.

First, I had to deal with those areas of anger and bitterness—and even hatred toward my tormentor/boss—in my heart. It became clear that my priorities needed adjusting so that my career was not such a huge idol in my life. Meanwhile, I had used those lonely wee hours in a dark house when I came home from work as an opportunity to write fiction, which eventually turned into my first book, *October Holiday*, which was published in 1993.

My second novel, *The Hofburg Treasures*, was published in 1995, and my third, *The Temple Scroll*, in 1996. These books were not so successful that I could make a living just writing fiction—unless I could magically accelerate the process to write seven or eight books a year. But they were enough of an encouragement that, when I was fired from my public relations job, I was not overly discouraged by not being able to find another PR position. It began to occur to me that maybe it was providential—an opportunity to try self-employment.

I would never have had the courage to up and quit the security of a steady, well-paying job with a wife and four kids to pursue a dream like that. But being fired was another matter. Then, not finding another replacement job persuaded me to give freelancing a try. Some of the jobs I investigated paid so meagerly that I knew I could do at least *that* well on my own. Thus was born Adams Business Communications, a one-man writing, editing, and public relations service, and a joint venture in management consulting services with a friend/partner.

The crowning irony, which really seemed to confirm the rightness of this approach, was that my former employer eventually became my biggest client. Looking back once again, I am reminded of the words of a U.S. President, a job counselor, and the angel of the Lord. Franklin D. Roosevelt said in the midst of America's worst depression that the only thing to fear was fear itself. Rick Crow of Cuyahoga County Reemployment Services defined *fear* this way: False Evidence Appearing Real.

Or, as the angel of the Lord said more simply, "Fear not."

For me, the first battle was casting out anger and fear. (They're really the flip side of each other.) After that, everything else began to fall into place. And, oh yes, one more fruit was produced out of the suffering process:

You're holding it in your hands. Fear not.

ACKNOWLEDGMENTS

I am greatly indebted to the following people for all of their kindness and assistance, without which *Reinventing Your Career* would never have been possible: Daniel Adams, Mary Jane Adams, Tony Ciepiel, Larry McNamee, Sam Lombardo, Debbie Kubacki, Dick Hanscom, Marlin Rupp, Bob Lucas, and Mike Donahoe. Also: Rick Crow and Bob Paponetti, at the Cuyahoga County Reemployment Services Center; Linda Walters at the Cuyahoga County Public Library; Martin Jaffe and Kathleen Savage at InfoPLACE; and Fred Yetka, Beverly Foster, Kande Koogle, Bobbi Umbach, and Marcia Venus at Right Associates.

ACKNOWLEDGMENTS

1   THE JOB SQUEEZE

I n Floyd Kemske's novel *Lifetime Employment*, a couple of employees of a high-tech company encounter the hero, Gene, on the elevator. It doesn't take long to see this is not your typical elevator conversation about the weather. "We want you to kill Larry," says one of them, referring to the chief of information systems.

Gene is taken aback, but less than one might expect. "I'll have to get back to you on that," he says, edging away from the employees. The reader wonders if Gene is just stalling or whether he first has to do a cost/benefit analysis on Larry.

At this company, the employees literally climb over the bodies of their co-workers to advance their own careers. Permanent job security is just a shot away for the victors. In a sense, the victims are actually the first—and maybe the only ones for sure—to achieve lifetime employment. It's just that their lifetimes are somewhat shorter than the norm.

In another Kemske novel, *Virtual Boss*, a business

firm has so decentralized that the only actual authority is a computer program—a bundle of interactive artificial intelligence software. It learns from its employee interactions and adapts its responses to facilitate peak performance from the myriad individual personalities. For one person, that may mean simple encouragement. For another, it may mean turning his life into a living hell. The virtual boss is more than willing to accommodate—and for some workers, hell it is.

And in *Human Resources,* Kemske pictures a corporate turnaround expert who comes to Biomethods, Inc., spouting all the latest jargon about "tearing down walls" and reengineering the corporation. Translation: Rip out an organization's guts, close down entire departments, and send longtime employees packing. So, that's fiction? In this case, the turnaround expert is also a vampire—a boss who figuratively *and* literally sucks the life out of employees. The vampire/boss, named Pierce, also guts a project seeking a cure for AIDS in favor of a different scheme to identify people's buying patterns by a blood test. Much better for the bottom line.

Kemske's novels would be good choices for a time capsule. Their satirically exaggerated picture of life in the waning months and years of the twentieth century would be a wonderful, though macabre, find for future archaeologists curious about today's phenomenon of dispensable workers and disposable people.

Except for the vampire, the Biomethods story is the all-too-familiar scenario of downsizings and mass layoffs/firings that haunts today's headlines. So-called human resources are being consumed like cords of wood, veins of ore, and carloads of coal. And, like the old vilified strip mines, the landscape is left scarred and littered with the detritus of human lives—living, breathing people who can give plaintive interviews to the *New York Times* and whose cries can be heard on the six o'clock news.

The strip mines have been largely shut down and

cleaned up. And while the world is being made safe for whales, baby seals, snail darters, and spotted owls, what about the human beings? Who will save them?

WHERE DID ALL THE JOBS GO?

Restructuring. Reengineering. Severance programs. Buyouts. Downsizing. Rightsizing. Delayering. Flattening. Process redesign. Reduction in force. Resource reallocation. It all adds up to the same thing: disappearing jobs. An employment black hole across America.

A half-million Americans a year are laid off, some of them thrown permanently out of work. And, according to a *New York Times* survey,

- Nearly three-quarters of all families have had a "close encounter" with layoffs since 1980.

- One-third of all U.S. households have a family member who has been laid off, and nearly 40 percent know a relative, friend, or neighbor who's been laid off.

- One in ten adults—or 19 million people—acknowledged that a lost job in his household "precipitated a major crisis" in his life.[1]

Only a generation ago, it was common for workers to have one career and not unusual even to have the same job all their working days. Lifetime employment was the norm. Today, experts say, the average person has about ten jobs in a lifetime and three career changes. Tomorrow—i.e., the turn of the century—they say it will be common for people to have six to ten *career changes* in their lives.

It is tempting to wring our hands in exasperation as if some fixed point in the universe suddenly has fallen out of orbit when, in fact, quite the opposite may be the case. In the scheme of things, jobs are a recent phenomenon. Work itself is as old as the first patch of weeds in the Garden after the Fall. But the packaging of work in the form of *jobs* is a mere two hundred years old—and a pendulum swing that may be in full reverse.

William Bridges, author of *JobShift: How to Prosper in a World Without Jobs*, calls jobs a "social artifact" of the industrial era.[2] Unfortunately, those of us who depend on this social artifact for many of our needs are living in what's been called the *Post*-Industrial Era.

"The job concept emerged early in the nineteenth century to package the work that needed doing in the growing factories and bureaucracies of the industrializing nations," wrote Bridges. "Before people had jobs, they worked just as hard but on shifting clusters of tasks, in a variety of locations, on a schedule set by the sun, the weather, and the needs of the day. The modern job was a startling new idea—to many people, an unpleasant and even socially dangerous one."[3]

IT WASN'T ALWAYS LIKE THIS

The Industrial Revolution began powering up in England and Western Europe shortly after the American Revolution in the late eighteenth century with such breakthroughs as steam-powered spinning machines and looms. Until then, the workplace had been the village, the field, and the home, where farmers, craftsmen, and families did their work without time clocks, employment contracts, and management consultants. Now the factory with its regimentation began to become the norm.

By the early twentieth century, another principle came to the fore—narrow functional specialization and scientific management, as defined by Frederick Taylor, the father of management gurus. This involved breaking jobs down into a large number of simple tasks the worker would repeat over and over with machine-like efficiency under a command-and-control type of supervision. Ironically, today's management consultants counsel quite different approaches—self-directed work teams, participative management, etc. Different times call for different prescriptions.

By 1914, Henry Ford introduced the assembly line, dividing tasks into narrow functional specialties and ushering in the era of mass production. It was the ideal means of manufacturing goods in great quantity with a large population of low-skilled and uneducated workers, many of them immigrants. Companies could train an individual to perform the same job routine repeatedly without requiring a great deal of independent thought. That was left to the growing cadre of supervisory and support personnel.

Under this approach, the United States became the manufacturing giant of the world—the largest producer and exporter of goods with the largest labor force and the highest wages. This remarkable success gave America the highest standard of living in the world, but the U.S. occupation of the catbird seat was far from permanent. The golden era of dominance, according to historians and economists, lasted approximately thirty years, from the end of World War II to the onset of the global economy and the Technology Revolution—1945 to 1975.

The illusion of permanent prosperity coincided with the advent of the baby boomer generation—76 million babies born from 1946 to 1964. The 1960s, though overshadowed by the threat of nuclear war, began with the glow of a Camelot presidency and the belief that America could "bear any burden, pay any price," in the words of John F. Kennedy. Expectations couldn't have been higher. Until her military might became bogged down in Vietnam, it seemed there was little that was not within America's grasp. President Kennedy vowed that America would put a man on the moon before the end of the decade. And, though Kennedy did not live to see it himself, the promise was fulfilled in 1969, when Neil Armstrong took a giant leap for mankind.

Economically, too, America was a juggernaut. But

success begat complacency, and without serious competition from abroad—at first—there was little incentive for U.S. manufacturers to worry about down-the-road problems with cost and quality. It became the age of inflation, as workers and companies pursued an upward spiral that eluded President Nixon's wage and price controls. But around the corner lurked two other major forces—consumerism and the quality movement.

Ralph Nader's career as a consumer advocate and corporation basher was launched with the publishing in 1972 of *Unsafe at Any Speed*, an indictment of U.S. automakers for shoddy design and workmanship, as evidenced by General Motors' less than stellar Corvair. Unwittingly, American manufacturers were setting themselves up as juicy targets once the Japanese and others figured out that they could beat the Yanks at their own game and capture a major portion of the global market with lower-cost, higher-quality goods.

Experts say the wake-up call began in 1973 with the Arab oil embargo, which decisively demonstrated that no nation—not even the U.S.A.—can go it alone and that the price of industrial might is energy dependence. The so-called global economy began to take center stage with the fall of Communism and the unification of Europe under the European Union, once called the European Economic Community. Then the Western Hemisphere followed suit with the removal of trade barriers through the North American Free Trade Agreement, whose opponents argued bitterly that it would cost U.S. jobs.

Foreign competition was one of four factors cited by the *New York Times* in a March 1996 series, "The Downsizing of America." The other three: stunning technological progress that lets machines replace hands and minds, the ease of contracting out work, and payroll cuts to make companies more attractive on Wall Street. To these could be added a generation of baby boomer managers much more willing than the previous generation to trim staff size, and changes in the accounting practices mandated by law.

THE TECHNOLOGY REVOLUTION

The Technology Revolution began a sharp spike in 1976 with the appearance of the personal computer, which offered the promise of putting mainframe power into the hands of ordinary people. Over the next twenty years, the PC began to redefine the workplace, changing the speed of work and the way literally thousands of different kinds of tasks are carried out. By the 1980s, power was doubling and the price was being cut in half approximately every eighteen months. By the 1990s, automakers were pointing out that the brains of their cars were bigger than the computers aboard the Apollo spacecraft.

But this new technology also was beginning to do something else a little less user-friendly: The long-feared specter of automation finally was taking its toll on jobs through industrial robots, computerized machinery, and microelectronic techniques. Soon, even white-collar workers, who had been immune to such vicissitudes in the past, began to fall prey to the pink slip as even those jobs began to disappear.

As long as computers have been around, the greater wonder may be why it's taken so long for this revolution to begin chopping heads. The answer may involve the ways technology is handled or, especially in the early stages, mishandled. Experts have noted that when the electric motor was first introduced, it took a remarkably long time to change things and fulfill its potential of portable power. At first, it was used simply as a direct replacement for the giant, smoky steam engine that had no place on the factory floor. Its power was transmitted instead to individual machines and work stations through a Rube Goldberg series of belts and pulleys connected to one central driveshaft from the outside.

Eventually, the industrial engineers figured out that there was a more efficient way of doing things, and the next technological corner was turned. Similarly, it wasn't until recent years that the power of computing reached critical mass in the workplace in a very direct human sense. Harry S. Dent, Jr., author of *JobShock*, said the tendency at first was to use information technology merely to enhance the old ways of the "paper-shuffling bureaucracy" rather than advance real innovation. Hence the older-generation manager whose desktop computer was little more than a high-tech paperweight. But that's all changing with a vengeance, Dent suggested in a section of his book entitled "Computers Are the New Office Workers."

"Sure, we've had computers in offices," he wrote,

> but we haven't used them to real advantage in most organizations. The workplace has been filled with an older generation used to working in a hierarchical command and control system. This generation is less willing to take risks than the newer generation moving into positions of power now and in the future: baby boomers. The members of this newer generation have already proved they will take necessary, calculated risks to bring in new, creative ways of conducting business when they have come into power.[4]

John Naisbitt and Patricia Aburdene, authors of *Megatrends*, accurately forecast the current situation more than a decade ago in their book *Re-inventing the Corporation*, when they predicted a major flattening of the ranks of middle managers in America. Staff managers who supervise people would give way to small groups, work teams, and other self-management structures, according to Naisbitt and Aburdene, and line managers in charge of systems would be replaced by computers.

Their words, published in 1985, seem eerily prophetic now:

Today, computers are replacing middle managers at a much greater rate than robots are replacing assembly line workers. Once indispensable to senior executives, many middle managers are now watching computers do their job in a fraction of the time and at a percentage of the cost. The whittling away of middle management presents serious problems for all those baby boomers about to enter middle management. The number of men and women between thirty-five and forty-six, the prime age range for entering middle management, will increase 42 percent between 1985 and 1995. Clearly, millions of baby boomers who aimed for middle management will never reach their goal. There simply will not be enough middle management jobs. It is a scary thought for some people.[5]

And that's pretty much what's happened. Various sources agree: The tables have been turned. The majority of laid-off workers now are college-educated, salaried employees who held white-collar jobs. It's a fact that helps account for the way the layoff/firing phenomenon is getting more national attention and publicity even though, in hard numbers, unemployment is not up, despite all the publicity.

PREDATORY LAYOFFS

That's not to say that all of the angst is simply inevitable. People wonder why so many people are losing their jobs if the economy is really as healthy as the experts say.

Clearly, some of the misery has been callously inflicted by a new breed of results-driven decision-makers whose primary motivation is the bottom line, shareholders' demands, and the daily ticker. Alan Downs, a former layoff specialist—"corporate executioner"—for several large corporations, points out in his book *Corporate Executions* that the term *layoffs* is worse than a euphemism. It's an outrageous misnomer for what in many cases is outright mercenary slaughter.

Downs says the term *layoff* implies that the job loss-es were unavoidable as a matter of corporate survival—i.e., the company had run out of work or out of money to pay its employees.[6] That's quite different from what he calls today's "binge-and-purge" staffing, in which the organization, like a bulimic, tries to disgorge itself of excess baggage for short-term gains, even at the expense of the long-term health of the organization—not to mention the lives and careers of its own employees.[7] *Layoff* also implies that these job losses are temporary when, in fact, no callback is even contemplated.

Downs tells the story of a defense contractor that offered its key executives bonuses equal to twice their annual salary in 1991 if the company's stock price could be jacked up from $25 to $45 a share for at least ten days. Not surprisingly, the managers found a way—by laying off 12,000 of the company's 86,000 employees.[8] Wall Street investors loved it, and the executives profited handsomely, but studies show that the gains of such strategies are gener-ally short-lived. In fact, like an athlete on steroids, the long-term health of the organization often suffers.

NEW ACCOUNTING STANDARDS

One of the typical worries of a laid-off employee's spouse is benefits—particularly the health plan. One cata-strophic medical problem can wipe out an entire family. One of the leading causes of personal bankruptcy is monu-mental medical bills. But even here, old-style corporate security is an illusion. Just look at what's happened over the past decade.

A few years ago, the national Financial Accounting Standards Board adopted new standards requiring compa-nies to begin accounting for things such as retiree health benefits directly on the books as outstanding liabilities. This most directly affected older, larger corporations, such as the big automakers, that had nearly as many retirees on their books as active employees. Putting those costs on the books was not a pretty sight. As costs escalated, companies began changing from defined benefits to defined contributions in order to cap their liability. In other words, instead of guaranteeing "first-dollar" coverage of all employees' health needs, they are now offering "X" dollars toward coverage. Employee premium-sharing is now the norm in America.

Guess which direction this trend is going? Hint: First-dollar coverage isn't about to make a comeback. In fact, employees can only expect to see more and more cost-sharing on their part—co-pays, deductibles, premium participation—and more restricted managed care type of plans—health maintenance organizations (HMOs), preferred provider organizations (PPOs), etc., in the future. There is even a movement to abandon the traditional risk pool in favor of every-man-for-himself type medical savings accounts that would function like medical IRAs. Clearly, the mood is in the direction of untying the employee from organizational custody.

A NEW SOCIAL CONTRACT

Cliff Hakim, an executive career consultant, wrote in *We Are All Self-Employed* that a new social contract has replaced the old employment paradigm. "Dependence on the organization is obsolete. The familiar employee-employer contract has now been broken. Loyalty to the organization no longer guarantees job security. Workplaces en masse are reshaping themselves to survive and compete, and millions of individuals have lost their jobs."[9]

Companies recognize this on one level but not on another, and so exhibit institutional schizophrenia, unintentionally sending mixed signals to their workforce. On one hand, they are still exercising old strategies that management consultant David Noer calls "person capturing"— offering benefit plans, recreation programs, group travel benefits, day care, tuition reimbursement plans, comprehensive career planning, raises and promotions by seniority and tenure—originally designed to tie the person to the organization and to be prepared for a predictable future.[10] On the other hand, the new reality is that organizations are really in the process of *un*tying employees in the face of an *un*predictable future. Their formal culture, i.e., what they profess, is not in sync with their own operational culture, i.e., what they actually *do*. In fact, it is even contradictory.

Reality has not entirely caught up with actual practice. Between the idea and the reality, wrote poet T. S. Eliot, falls the shadow. In these times we are living in the shadowlands.

NO TURNING BACK

But when we emerge from the shadowlands, the employees who acknowledge the new reality will be well ahead toward coping with it and even thriving. Having a traditional job, a regular paycheck, and fringe benefits breeds a kind of security-mindedness that crushes the spirit and rots the bones when it's withheld—*entitlement*. Part of the current media-stoked angst is an assumption that, as Americans, we have been deprived of some fundamental birthright in all of this economic upheaval. It's the glass-is-half-empty attitude instead of "God's grace shed on thee" when compared with the standard of living almost anywhere else in the world.

Judith M. Bardwick, a management consultant and psychologist, says entitlement results when people "don't have to earn what they get" and soon "take for granted what they receive." In *Danger in the Comfort Zone* she said the entitlement disease is not just a rap against lower-level workers. It's also hard at work among high-level corporate executives of large organizations that "freeze wages, lay workers off, and give executives big raises."[11]

Paradoxically, this "danger in the comfort zone,"

according to Bardwick, is at its greatest when "life is too safe." Considering the current turmoil and upheaval, could that mean America is actually becoming healthier? Could it be that Americans need to recover some of the self-reliance and God-reliance that made the United States great? Has too much of this reliance been transferred to the organization?

"By protecting people from risk, we destroy their self-esteem," Bardwick wrote. "We rob them of the opportunity to become strong, competent people. Facing risk is the only way we gain confidence, because confidence is the result of mastering challenge. Confidence is an internal state. It cannot be given; it can only be earned. The only way to get genuinely confident is to be familiar with fear and then conquer it."[12]

David Noer gives similar advice in a discussion of what he calls *layoff survivor sickness*, his description of the effects on organizations of contemporary downsizing. In *Healing the Wounds*, Noer says that workers who survive the ax become demotivated, feeling "a deep sense of violation." And their organizations often fail to reap the touted benefits for all that pain.

> Organizations that once saw people as assets to be nurtured and developed began to view those same people as costs to be cut. . . . Organizations institute layoffs to cut costs and promote competitiveness but afterward often find themselves worse off than before. All they have gained is a depressed, anxious, and angry workforce. At the very time they need spirit and creativity, they enter into global competition with a risk-averse team.[13]

Noer says a major part of the survivor sickness is denial—going on with business as usual as if nothing has changed when, in fact, things are never going to be the same. Workers must approach employment with a less dependent and more autonomous, entrepreneurial attitude in the future, especially in assessing their own self-worth, Noer says. "Don't place your spiritual currency in the organizational vault," he writes.[14]

But how, exactly, does one change something as fundamental as one's attitudes and self-image? Perhaps a lead can be taken from the plethora of American enterprises that similarly have found their very existence threatened until they changed the fundamental nature of their business.

The electronics giant Motorola, for example, was in such a situation in the 1970s. Those were the days when Steve Allen starred in television commercials for Motorola's Quasar TV, touting the technological marvel of its "works in a drawer" for easy repair. Unfortunately, this was the same time that Japanese companies such as Sony were conquering the TV market with Zero Defects products. Easy repair is a hands-down loser to no repair every time. Motorola soon was out of the TV business.

To their credit, Motorola's executives rose to the occasion and salvaged the situation by changing product lines. Now the company is the world's leading manufacturer of communications devices and a leading computer chip maker, and its encounter with the defects issue was a hard lesson well learned. Today Motorola is a leader in the Total Quality movement and has made "Six Sigma" variance a well-known standard for excellence.

In these turbulent times numerous businesses have had to make radical changes to survive. They have had to reinvent themselves. And individuals may have to do much the same thing—reinvent their careers.

It's time to meet a few people who have had to rise to the occasion.

NOTES

1. "The Downsizing of America," *New York Times*, series, March 3 to March 9, 1996.

2. William Bridges, *JobShift: How to Prosper in a World Without Jobs* (Reading, Mass.: Addison-Wesley, 1994), viii.
3. Ibid.
4. Harry S. Dent, Jr., *JobShock: Four New Principles Transforming Our Work and Business* (New York: St. Martin's, 1995), 7.
5. John Naisbitt and Patricia Aburdene, *Re-inventing the Corporation: Transforming Your Job and Your Company for the New Information Society* (New York: Warner, 1985), 14.
6. Alan Downs, *Corporate Executions* (New York: Amacom, 1995), 7.
7. Ibid., 13.
8. Ibid., 25–26.
9. Cliff Hakim, *We Are All Self-Employed: Achieving Independence, Collaboration, and Fulfillment Inside or Outside Organizations* (San Francisco: Berrett-Koehler, 1994), 13. David M. Noer, in *Healing the Wounds: Overcoming the Trauma of Layoffs and Revitalizing Downsized Organizations* (San Francisco: Jossey-Bass, 1993), 143, makes a similar point, as does Alan Downs in *Corporate Executions,* 206–7. Downs's work on this subject is discussed in chapter 9 of this book, "Alternatives."
10. Noer, *Healing the Wounds,* 139.
11. Judith M. Bardwick, *Danger in the Comfort Zone: From Boardroom to Mailroom: How to Break the Entitlement Habit That's Killing American Business* (New York: Amacom, 1991), 18–19.
12. Ibid., 28.
13. Noer, *Healing the Wounds,* xv.
14. Ibid., 151.

2

DISPOSABLE PEOPLE

I f a company produced leading-edge technology, there was a good chance that **Ri Regina** worked for it at some point through the 1970s and 1980s. Her résumé was a virtual "Who's Who" of technology and information companies—Opinion Research Corp., Hewlett-Packard, Royal Business Machines, Wang Laboratories, Lexis/Nexis. Ri—short for "Maria"—had been involved in product marketing and management in the early development stage of CD-ROM technology in 1984.

Her growing reputation and opportunities as a manager in the information industry were heady stuff, including such perks as dinner at Bill Gates's home. By the 1990s, the now-familiar corporate upheavals were becoming inescapable. After a downsizing reorganization at Lexis/Nexis in 1993 cut her team significantly and soured the work environment, she decided to move on yet again. By 1994, she said, "I started looking around, because my feeling was I don't want to stay here with this atmosphere and this sort of anxiety-inducing environment outside."

So, she put her "sheet on the street"—i.e., her résumé. Through her now sizable network, she found a job at AT&T GIS (Global Information Solutions) in Dayton, Ohio. The company, better known as NCR Corp. before it was acquired in a hostile takeover in 1991 by AT&T, was the old National Cash Register company, for generations a pillar of the Miami Valley economy. Ri went there in August 1994 as director of multimedia marketing, a senior management position that included trips to Europe and more cutting-edge technology development, including desktop video and electronic imaging.

"We're talking any sort of imaging," she said, "an image database where you could go in and, for example, do a scan for a particular set of eyes so that if you had a terrorist coming through an airport, you could scan the eyes and then compare the eyes of each individual coming off the plane with the database of eyes that had certain multimedia characteristics, that sort of stuff. We had the multimedia kiosks, where you had video information for selling or training or presenting. It was all over the board, and it was broadband technology. It was an incredible raw set of technology and concepts."

But this time the career story had a different ending. The bullet Ri had dodged in Boston found its mark in Dayton. She was told her group was being dissolved August 15, 1995, a little over a year after coming there and two weeks after her husband, Bob, a computer software and hardware engineer, started a new job in Cincinnati. Nationwide, AT&T was in the process of divesting itself of some forty thousand employees. By October 1995, the reorganization in Dayton turned into permanent layoffs for some 1,100 employees—including Ri. She said it was surprisingly traumatic.

"It's funny," Ri said, "because I knew it was coming, and I was prepared for it. Psychologically, OK, I am part of the layoff, and I am not getting the offers from (other departments) within AT&T which I would have expected. What's going on here? It was almost this feeling of 'What's wrong with me?' And you sort of teeter on the edge of starting to feel bad about yourself. How can they lay me off? I am special. I know about these other people. I can understand why they laid them off, but why would they ever lay *me* off?"

She said the silver lining was the assistance she received from the national outplacement firm Right Associates as part of her severance. At her level in the corporation, she was entitled to six months of outplacement assistance at the agency, which provided both job counseling and physical office facilities for the job search process in a positive and supportive environment.

"It really helped to have an office to go to and a schedule of meetings every single day and a process to follow and work to be done," said Ri. "In terms of handling my sense of rejection, a lot of the sessions that we went to at Right Associates really centered on identifying your worth, identifying your value, identifying your unique skill set, and recognizing the business necessity that the company faced in having to get rid of X amount of dollars, as opposed to getting rid of *you*, the person. It is almost as if you could say, 'I was a high-dollar employee—of course, you were going to lay me off.' So it was almost your red badge of courage."

※ ※ ※

Mel Marsh had worked for NCR for fifteen years in a wide variety of positions before the downsizing. She was the director of the office of technology planning, and her job was called "innovation consultant." "Mel" is short for "Melinda."

"I helped specific organizations be more innovative and focus what we were doing in trying to develop a technology plan," she said. "We applied innovation, working with the technology experts and helping them think a bit outside the box as to how could we apply these different technologies—what technologies should we be involved in five, ten, or fifteen years down the road."

Her outlook was fundamentally different from Ri's. After much soul-searching during the summer of 1995, when the layoff plans were disclosed, Mel decided to put her own neck on the block. "I said, 'Do I want to stay or do I want to take this opportunity to start my own company?'" If the severance payment was large enough, it might work.

She said it was something she had been thinking about for quite some time anyway. "I wanted to have a whole lot more control over my life, and I had a great deal of disappointment with corporate America. There is a lot of push for people to get things done, and then when you get something done or almost done, all of a sudden it isn't needed anymore. You put your heart and soul into a project, and then the project dies. I just decided that I was tired of putting my heart and soul into something and watching it fall down the tubes. I would rather put my heart and soul into something I could actually nurture and grow."

So, she took a deep breath and offered to walk the plank. "I made my decision and told my boss and said I would really like to go."

The offer was accepted.

※ ※ ※

Roy Peterson (not his real name) was director of human resources development for a large Ohio insurance company.

"I was responsible for all of the education as well as organizational and cultural change for the entire corporation," he said. "Claims training, customer service training, sales training, information systems; supervisory, management and executive development organization survey work; and Total Quality Process implementation and the skill sets required to make that happen—measurement skills."

Roy's company also decided to downsize as part of a reengineering program. In this case, most of it would be done via voluntary severance packages. Like Mel Marsh, Roy could have availed himself of a golden parachute. His employer encouraged middle manager types to take the offers, warning that failure to do so could result in termination without a severance package.

Roy felt he had been an integral part of a successful renaissance for the company. "The organization tried to shift itself from an old-style, 1950s or 1960s autocratic sort of place to a much more open, involved, empowered, participative type of place and had been very successful," he said. In fact, in the last six years the company pulled itself up from next to last among its peer group companies nationally to the top five in terms of service performance and posted its most profitable year ever.

What Roy didn't know was that the company had some additional plans in mind as well. "I think that the decision was to set the company up to sell it, which is what eventually happened," he said. "I think that was what drove the downsizing and outsourcing."

Before the company was sold, it eliminated about five hundred employees through the voluntary severance program and then a few dozen more in selected departments later through outright discharge. Roy took a gamble that he would dodge the bullet. By October 1995 he was history.

"I let the voluntary severance pass me by and took a chance of being outright discharged—and I got discharged," he said. "That's exactly what happened."

And unlike Mel Marsh, it was most definitely not OK, especially at first.

"It was absolutely and unequivocally earth-shattering," he said. "It was the one thing in life that I foolishly assumed would never happen to me. It always happened to someone else, of course, and it did happen to me. And it really shook pretty deep for quite some time, actually, and I had to struggle a lot to get to a point that I was able to deal with it fairly reasonably. It was not the best week of my life; it was a pretty lousy week."

※ ※ ※

At Cleveland's WJW-TV Channel 8, **Bob "Casey" Kasarda** was not caught totally unawares when the ax fell. He'd already been moonlighting for some time as a videographer and commercial video producer. In fact, he'd made a major purchase of equipment by coincidence only a few weeks before.

Casey was at Channel 8 for twenty-eight years, sixteen years as a news photographer and then twelve years as a videographer for an evening feature program called "PM Magazine." By 1986 he and his wife, Marianne, had four children in college and a growing need for additional income. So he bought a camera and began doing freelance work, largely corporate videos for companies in Ohio, Michigan, Pennsylvania, and West Virginia. As this side work grew, Casey decided to organize it as a part-time family-owned business and called it Gemini Productions, Inc. Since all four kids were studying either radio and television or marketing, advertising, and communications, it made sense.

Casey had no idea at the time how providential that decision would prove to be. For one thing, by the time his eldest son graduated from college, the job market had become glutted with candidates attracted to the supposed glamor of television production. "When Jeff got out of school, there were lines of people trying to get into TV stations," he said. Employment was more likely to be found in the commercial production studios, like larger versions of Gemini.

DISPOSABLE PEOPLE ———————————————— 41

For another thing, "PM Magazine" was about to be canceled. Over the years, the staff had become a tight-knit family of professionals who respected each other. "I traveled the world with 'PM Magazine,'" said Casey. "We were in Australia, New Zealand, Portugal, Switzerland, Ireland. . . . Everyone got along. We all had good things to say about one another. We all understood each other's problems and needs, and it was a great show."

First, the station replaced "PM Magazine" with "Cleveland Tonight," which was locally produced at Channel 8 by Casey and his associates. That bought another year's lease on life. Meanwhile, things were still happening in quadruples in the Kasarda family. In just slightly over a year—from April 1989 to May 1990—all the Kasarda kids were getting married.

Then in August 1990 the other shoe dropped. "Cleveland Tonight" was being canceled too. Casey and another dozen Channel 8 staffers received their pink slips, and they were gone. As busy as he had become with Gemini Productions, there was somewhat of a delayed reaction before the full impact sank in.

"The next day I really got upset and realized what had happened," he said. "I was fifty-one. Another nine more years and I could have retired at Channel 8. When you spend pretty much your career life at one place . . ."

Never one to wear his emotions on his sleeve, Casey left the thought unfinished.

※ ※ ※

Don Kennedy, sixty-three, is also in the twilight of his career as an engineer and business executive. In his case, the pink slips came in quadruplicate. He lost a succession of jobs in the rubber injection molding industry as three different Cleveland companies were sold out from under him and a fourth just didn't work out. Don puts the finger of blame on global competition.

"All of these companies had bearing down on them products that were worldwide in their ultimate market, and, therefore, they were vulnerable to worldwide competition," he said. "This was not true in the 1930s, '40s, '50s, and '60s, when everyone could make everything and you could sell everything you made. But as the world got smaller, in effect because of communications, survival became the name of the game rather than to make a better product, more of squeezing costs and eliminating positions."

Don said the combination of global competition and changing technology has all but ended career opportunities in this country for engineers such as himself.

"In the rubber injection molding field, as worldwide manufacturers bear down on the marketplace in the United States, ninety-five percent of the manufacturers are foreign, and that used to be the reverse when I first started out of college. The United States has not kept up to the manufacturing capabilities of other countries. So, today our competition is Austrian, German, and Italian. The market now is shifting not only overseas, but it is increasingly more plastic rather than rubber. The market that I have known for twenty to thirty years is slowly disappearing."

He said he ended up with no pension from any of the companies he worked for and will face retirement with only what he and his wife have managed to save. But Don is not overly discouraged. Since losing his last job in December 1995, he has managed to find a variety of other short-term and part-time jobs, most recently working with a graphic design company while helping his former employer one week a month. But he does have some concern for the next generation.

"I have to think from what I hear that we are going to see many more changes for our children," he said. "Their careers are not going to be as stable as our parents' were. You'd better be light on your feet now."

❈ ❈ ❈

It wasn't a market shakeout that cost **Carol Bloom** her job, but changes in the publishing industry certainly complicated her finding another position when things went south. Carol was publications director of an international honor society in education at a university town in Indiana. The clashes with her boss started almost immediately, only worsened over time, and eventually cost her her job.

"My management style was team coach; his was family patriarch," she said. "We were a deadly mismatch." Despite her department's growing success and national acclaim for its publications, Carol was fired in November 1995 after three and a half years. In her own words:

"The morning I was fired seemed set at a different speed. I arrived, I met my supervisor in his office, and within minutes I was typing up a resignation letter. If I refused to resign, I would receive no severance, only my current paycheck. If I resigned and signed a waiver that I would not take any legal action against my supervisor or the society, I would receive three months' severance. I hastily thought of my immediate need for survival and agreed to resign and sign the waiver. I have thought many times over whether I made the right decision, but my family would not have survived without my severance. I would not take further action, even filing for unemployment, because I respected the society and its leaders.

"After I turned in my resignation letter, I was given less than thirty minutes to call my husband (Bob), tell my staff, and leave the premises. I would return three separate evenings to pack up my belongings, which had merged with the department's since I had no intention of ever leaving. My husband was speechless, although he and I had discussed reasons for my early meeting with my supervisor the night before. Telling my staff was surreal. I had known I could not work for my supervisor forever, but I always thought he would be the one to tire of his position and leave. I would never be the one to leave. My staff was outraged and supportive; they were not sure what to do or say. Neither was I.

"I drove home stunned. My thoughts raced: I was no longer with this honor society. I would no longer be producing its publications. I was thrown out as unsuitable. I was angry and crushed. Luckily, I had plans to go to my national social studies teachers organization's annual conference the next day. I love to network because I love people, and rooming with an old friend and sharing my situation with empathetic colleagues calmed my worries and feelings of rejection and abandonment. I also saw several members of the honor society, who were incredulous at my fate and encouraging that I would land on my feet soon.

"But where *would* I land? What did I want to do? I had never planned to leave. Should I return to textbook publishing? Classroom teaching? Should we move to another city? My husband was up for a promotion to management, and neither of us relished moving again. I had not applied for a teaching license when we moved to this new state, so I could not teach or substitute, and I dreaded the corporate politics of the textbook publishing world. I knew I wanted to stay in publishing and preferably educational publishing."

The problem was a shrinking job market, as larger publishers continued to devour smaller ones. "With barely a handful of textbook publishers remaining," said Carol, "in-house staffs have shrunk significantly, and editorial management positions, which I would covet, would be few, very competitive, and centered in New York, Boston, or San Francisco, where our teenaged daughter's schooling and the cost of living would be concerns."

Her solution would have to involve the same independent-mindedness that had gotten her into trouble in the first place.

※ ※ ※

A simple change in management led to **Kay Hoff's** career crisis.

For the first two years as activity director for some fifteen hundred residents of a high-rise apartment building in the Cleveland suburb of Parma, she couldn't have been happier. She spent much of her time working with people at opposite ends of the age spectrum—seniors and children. For the adults there were bingo, crafts, coffee klatches, and day trips. For the children there were movies, games, outdoor activities, cookouts, and crafts. There was even a summer Junior Olympics—a basketball tournament for the junior high and senior high students.

"It was primarily a job designed to get the people at the apartments involved so that they felt that it was more of a home and less of an apartment environment," she said. "The company that owned the apartments wanted the people to feel that this was really a place where they wanted to continue to live for a long period of time instead of just a year or two."

Because she was both a licensed social worker and a certified public school teacher, it seemed like the perfect situation. "I thought I had the ideal job," she said. The last few months, ending in December 1994, were an entirely different story. She returned to work from a six-month medical leave in April 1994 to find that a new property manager had started in March. Suddenly, nothing was the same anymore.

Whereas before, Kay had used apartment volunteers to deliver fliers and newspapers to the units, now she was required to deliver them personally. "The very first day I came back off medical leave, having had foot surgery—the doctor had released me to go back to work—she (the property manager) informed me that I could no longer use volunteers and everything that was to be delivered I had to deliver personally door-to-door for three hundred sixty-five apartments."

Previously, the company had encouraged the use of volunteers to promote residents' involvement. "The people felt hurt because they enjoyed being involved," said Kay. "There are many people who live there that have no family and have nobody. They were just adding more work on top of it all just to see how much they could push me to see if maybe they could get me to break down and not be able to do the job."

There were other incidents, including write-ups and warnings over trivial matters, such as outdated cream cheese in a refrigerator, lack of soap in a bathroom, and even some things that occurred while she was on vacation. "I felt that if I quit my job, I was making an admission that I had done things wrong in my job—and I didn't believe I had," she said. "I had to fight myself every day to go to work. The property manager looked at me with hate. I could see it in her eyes. When they finally realized that I was not going to quit, on December 6, 1994, they called me in and fired me."

In exchange for promising not to sue, management would not contest her unemployment. Kay, a diabetic, felt they had been surprised when she returned from medical leave after her surgery and thought they could pressure her to quit. She felt a lawsuit would drag on too long, and she needed to get on with life. Her family needed the extra income.

"It really was devastating to me, because I loved my job very much, and I felt that I was very good at it, and I felt that I did a very conscientious job. And so, to have to go through seven months of pure misery and then finally to be fired was very devastating. I finally realized that I really in my heart believed that there was nothing I had done personally to get put into this position. I had to let it go or it would have driven me crazy.

"Those seven months had to be the worst time of my life. It was the longest time. It took a toll on my family, because it is very hard to go on from day to day to day and not have your family be affected by it. My faith helped because I believed that the Lord would help me and do what was going to be best for me in the long run."

A few months later, Kay's life was to change again. She was back in the hospital, this time for a partial leg amputation. Now she walks with a prosthesis. "What doesn't kill us makes us strong," she says with a smile. That's Kay Hoff.

And if this is all just a bit discouraging, if not depressing, stay tuned. That's not the end of the story.

3 STARTING OVER

osing a job is hard not to take personally. It feels like a personal rejection. Sometimes that's exactly what it is. Unfortunately, it usually doesn't end there, either. There's generally plenty more rejection in store for the average job prospector before he finds his pot of gold.

Richard S. Hanscom, Jr., operations director of Cleveland's Career Initiatives Center (CIC) for unemployed executives and managers, puts it this way: "Finding a job is the toughest work you will ever find. You will face rejection constantly."

Like the people he helps counsel, Hanscom has first-hand experience with rejection in the workplace. For seventeen years, Hanscom was vice president of production for Hough Bakeries, a family-owned business that was bought out by new owners. About three years before it finally went out of business, Hanscom was called in to the president's office at five o'clock on a Monday and told he was through.

"They said clean out your desk," he said, "and I was

watched, and in fifteen minutes I was out the door. I asked if I could go down to the production floor to say good-bye to the people, and they said no, and that was it. I talked to the supervisors and the people on the floor and they didn't want me around at all."

The kicker was that Hanscom unknowingly had been training his own replacement. "I had been training this guy for a year and a half to be my assistant, and when they thought he was ready—*bang*—I am out the door."

Hanscom became a client at the CIC as he contemplated how to salvage his career. "It was the roughest year of my life," he said. "It was terrible. Unemployment was awful. Not only is it the emotional thing; it is the financial thing. You can't live on unemployment. Fortunately, I had a wife who was working, and all the kids were just about through college. So we survived, but a lot of people don't. It affects the family structure. If the marriage was shaky, this will put an end to it. Lots of times the husband was the breadwinner, and as long as he was employed and there were some problems, they were overlooked. Once he becomes unemployed, these other problems become magnified."

Hanscom considered becoming a consultant or going into business for himself. "I didn't want to get back into the corporate world where someone could walk in any morning and say, 'I'm sorry we just don't need you anymore.'" Somewhere along the line he realized that the type of career counseling the CIC did was what really moved his heart. "This was the kind of support that managerial/professional people need. It was people helping each other." He figured out ways of increasing the membership and the budget and ended up being hired as its director.

Hanscom found his new career in the midst of confusion, adversity, and rejection, and his own experience gave him credibility. "You let people talk when they come in and let them vent their frustrations and all," he said, "and then you tell them you know where they are coming from because the same thing happened to you."

Rick Crow, a psychologist, career counselor, and former Catholic priest, shares a similar view on rejection. In fact, he teaches a program called "The Positive Side of Rejection."

"We view our inadequacy feelings as unique and deeply personal, and they are actually very universal," said Crow, case manager at the Cuyahoga County Reemployment Services Center. "Rejection gets easier with practice. You weave it into a certain kind of success percentage about what you are doing. The more you practice, the better you get at it, like anything else. The apprehension of rejection is almost worse than the actual occurrence—worrying about, thinking about, and anticipating it. There really are no failures, only learning experiences and opportunities, and it is what you choose it to be.

"What I teach and what I try to practice myself is that blaming doesn't do anything. What I tell people is that if you are going to blame or if you are going to feel sorry for yourself, set aside fifteen minutes a day to do it, and when the fifteen minutes are up, get back to life. Take time out if you have to brood or if you have to blame, but it is really not doing anything but ventilating. Do that and get the poison out. Be conscious of when you are letting other people determine your behavior. Be aware of whether you are a determiner or a reactor, so that you can know when you are doing one or the other."

And now back to our previous case studies, for the rest of the story.

CAREER REINVENTORS

After some exposure at Right Associates to the concept of starting her own business, **Ri Regina** decided this might be the solution to putting her "sheet on the street" and uprooting her family yet again. The only thing she knew was that any such business venture would definitely involve leading-edge technology. "I have been so fortunate throughout my whole career to always be working on the new technology stuff right when it is just coming out," she said.

Then almost out of the blue an opportunity came along that "dumbfounded and delighted" her. A former boss at Lexis/Nexis was trying to launch an Internet services business and needed a full partner. She thought of Ri and invited her to join. Ri's only hesitation was whether she could afford to forgo the kind of income she was accustomed to at large corporations in order to launch a start-up. After some bottom-line financial terms were worked out, a deal was struck, and they were in business.

Net Presence, Inc., provides Internet marketing and consulting services for businesses, including setting up Web sites on the World Wide Web and Internet training. A related line of business is an electronic commerce service called Buy It Online, which is a directory for products and services that can be purchased online. The potential rewards for an enterprise like Net Presence or Buy It Online are almost unlimited. So far, the short-term rewards haven't been bad either. By midyear 1996, Ri and her partner had covered their agreed minimum monthly needs for the rest of the year.

❊ ❊ ❊

After offering to take a voluntary severance from NCR, **Mel Marsh** has gone into business in an unlikely combination of services—management consulting and pottery.

"My company is Acorn Consulting," she said, "and I am specializing in the area of innovation and teamwork, helping organizations learn new skills so they can get themselves out of their problems in a slightly different fashion than they would have before. The reason for the teamwork is that one of the facts of life about creativity and innovation is that, if you have a hostile work environment, you will never be creative because your ideas will be shot down before you even have a chance to utter them. . . . I think I am going to be successful."

Across the patio at home is her other business, Mellow Pottery. "It is letting my artist out," she said. "I have a kiln, I have a wheel, I have a studio. So I do wheel-turned pottery. It was a hobby, and I decided, since it was a hobby and I had gotten good enough, that I might as well turn it into a business and pay for all that investment that I had in the hobby equipment."

She added, "It is not often that you can get someone to essentially finance the first couple months of your start-up. I know a lot of people who get laid off think about starting a business because they can't figure out if they are going to get another job, but I quit in order to start my own business, and this is absolutely the way I want to go.

"The time I have had in it so far has convinced me that this is absolutely well suited for my skills and my personality. Despite the fact that I am working more hours than I am used to, I still feel a great deal more control over what I am doing. And while I certainly understand that I am going to do major proposals and things like that that aren't going to pan out completely, that's OK. It comes with the territory. . . . This is absolutely how I plan to live the rest of my life until I retire."

※ ※ ※

Despite having taken it in the neck, **Roy Peterson** has been in the enviable position of having his cake and eating it too. In retrospect, the decision that was his undoing—taking a pass on the insurance company's voluntary severance program—proved to be a blessing in disguise.

Roy has started his own consulting service. The kicker is that his former employer is his biggest client.

"The bad news is they outsourced my job," he said. "The good news is I got the contract. Which means I get to continue to do a lot of the things I did and a number of things I did not, and I have an opportunity to work in a lot of other places. In a lot of respects, actually, I won on this one."

His former employer actually gave him six months to wrap up his job, which gave him time to plan. "In fact, before I left I had been asked if I would come back and begin to work on some things," said Roy. "That question would have never been posed had I taken the voluntary severance. They would have never asked me. There was some feeling in the corporation that those who took the severance were turning their backs and walking away and that sort of thing and were not showing any loyalty. If you took the buyout, you were history organizationally."

But that doesn't mean there aren't hard feelings on Roy's part. "Everyone goes through huge trauma. The one thing that I will never ever forgive the people that put me through this for is making my children cry. I will absolutely not forgive them for that. . . . The truth of the matter is there is a tremendous cost, and I don't know how much resentment a particular family might have. We had a lot."

Roy said that "the shrinking corporation is becoming a reality" through outsourcing and downsizing, but as a consultant he would recommend against it. "I would tell a company that they shouldn't downsize," he said. "Improved efficiency means that you can do more with the same number, and you are stupid to look at useful resources you have and get rid of them to become 'more efficient' in order to grow, in order to hire someone else back, and go through the process of training them all over again. That's dumb. That's long-term economic stupid."

But he would recommend the self-employed life to others. "I think most people ought to consider getting ready for it," Roy said. "There is a good side to being off on your own. It's pretty cool."

※ ※ ※

In one sense, it was almost a relief when **Bob Kasarda** got his pink slip from Channel 8. He was becoming increasingly torn between his regular job and his growing time commitment to his homegrown Gemini Productions. The discharge solved that problem, but now he was holding the bag on a major purchase of expensive production equipment—three-quarters of an entire editing suite. There was little choice: For better or worse, Gemini Productions was now his livelihood.

"Of course, if I had gotten laid off before, I would have never, never bought that equipment," said Casey. "I would have never taken the chance, but it just happened, and I felt everything would be OK." In fact, on the Monday after his Friday layoff, he was in West Virginia, already freelancing on another job.

"The problem I had been having," he said, "was trying to handle both jobs, because Gemini was starting to grow and, of course, I had all the time I had committed to Channel 8. It was hard to take up all that time. I was really getting concerned. I had a couple of major projects that I was doing for **BP** (British Petroleum) at that time, and I was concerned how I was going to meet the deadline dates, get everything videotaped that I needed to get videotaped, and handle the job at Channel 8. And probably when I got the notice, in a way it was a relief. It was a shock, as well, but not a stunning shock."

It helped that the terms of his discharge included a twenty-six-week severance package. But that didn't cover everything. Fortunately, he was able to borrow the rest from within the family. "We're still trying to pay that back," he said. Casey has few regrets, but he knows it's all in his hands. Not every day is a bed of roses. "Running a business is pretty difficult," he said.

Gemini now employs two of his children. His goal is to be able to leave something behind. "What I would like to see for Gemini Productions down the road," he said, "is that we become successful and we make a lot of money and I can retire and I could have my family take over the business and run it."

※ ※ ※

After his last job loss, **Don Kennedy** tried his hand at several different things out of his field of engineering and sales. He drove a cab for a week and decided that wasn't for him. He drove a downtown tour bus called "Lolly the Trolley," but the work was too seasonal. Finally, he ended up working for a publisher of professional journals, doing some graphic design and sales, while also working one week a month for his former employer.

"I kind of told them I thought they were foolish to dump me and that I had a lot of experience," he said, "and I kind of hinted that if they kept to their position, I was probably going to go to a competitor and lend them all of my contacts. So I think they had a chance to reflect on that." But eventually, Don plans to phase out the engineering work and go full-time with the publisher.

Don said he got an eyeful attending career counseling programs at both the Cuyahoga County Reemployment Services Center and the Career Initiatives Center. "It's a heartbreaker," he said, "because you will see men who have worked for one company for forty years, and they are walking into walls because they don't know what to do. They don't know how to shift gears. They are trying very hard, and they find themselves in their mid-fifties, overweight, not used to going and knocking on doors to get a job, and it is terribly sad to see it."

Nevertheless, Don maintains a dogged personal optimism. "Sometimes, one has to draw on either your spiritual side or your philosophy of life," he said. "I have been very fortunate that I have had many opportunities to think about why things happen to people, and nine times out of ten, if not even ten out of ten, the things that meant the most to me I never saw coming and never planned on. They just happened without any forethought on my part. Every change that I have ever had in my life has always meant an ultimately better position, and in most cases it was more money, but in this case right now it is more happiness."

❈ ❈ ❈

After taking a personal self-inventory, **Carol Bloom's** solution was to form her own venture, a full-service editorial company called Bloom Ink Publishing Professionals. "Because I loved project management, I could take on planning and creating a book, publication, annual report, or brochure from initial concept to final printed product," she said. Bloom Ink services would include copyediting, writing, proofreading, manuscript analysis, publication evaluation, consulting, and publications/print project management.

"Several of my friends who had left the textbook publisher were succeeding as independent contractors," she said. "So I interviewed them about the ups and downs of being in business for themselves. I learned that the flow of work was often feast and famine and that publishers paid better than the development houses often employed by publishers to handle editorial and production stages of teacher materials. Every freelancer I spoke to mentioned cash flow concerns—clients taking up to twelve weeks to pay for freelance services.

"Unlike me, most of these women loved the solitude of home as a workplace. Being very social and extroverted,

I feared that home would isolate me from human contact and loneliness would consume me. And indeed, after I had decided to take the risk of owning my own business, I did fight loneliness for the first two months."

The experience also resulted in some self-discovery. Still dealing with her own troubled emotions, Carol sought counseling.

"It has helped me immensely," she said of the counseling. "The hurt, anger, and loneliness dissipated as I talked about my feelings in being fired and its aftermath. I learned that the environment at the office was dysfunctional and the behavior of my supervisor resembled that of an alcoholic father. The employees were his children, each trying to stay out of his way, glad not to gain his attention for fear it would be a negative experience. When any one of us was in his favor, we enjoyed it cautiously, knowing we would soon enough be on the outs. By being direct and confrontational when a problem surfaced, I was forcing him to look at reality instead of the world he preferred to configure for us all.

"Because I was not willing to be a player in his charade, despite his respect for my abilities, with time he could no longer permit me to be a part of the family. Now knowing better how such a climate is maintained by a controlling person, I was better able to accept that I had little control over changing the environment, which I feared was my failing, and that it was best for my health and sanity that I was no longer a part of that office."

※ ※ ※

Kay Hoff was unemployed for about a year before things began to turn around. "I drew unemployment for six months," she said, "and when that ran out, things got tight, going to one income." Being confined to a wheelchair until she graduated to a prosthesis, she began praying for an opportunity to do something at home in a legitimate business, not a "rip-off kind of thing."

Several weeks later, she got a call from a friend that led to just such an opportunity. Almost before she knew it, Kay was working as the telephone contact for a company called Chestnut Prints, a small retailer of fine art, taking orders and selling prints. The owner, who worked as a tool and die maker by day, and his wife found out the hard way that people ordering art prints didn't want to deal with a recorded message on an answering machine.

"They realized by looking at their phone bill and their 800 numbers that their calls were only lasting seconds," Kay said. "A lot of people weren't even listening to the message. They didn't find someone there, so they hung up and called another art dealer. Especially when a gallery calls, they have a customer that wants a print, they have to get right on the phone and locate that print, and they have to get it sold before that customer cools off. They can't afford to have someone get back to them eight to ten hours later."

At first, the job was a little intimidating because Kay would have to quote prices to customers with only limited information on hand. Much of the company's sales was not from its own inventory, but from purchasing and reselling on the spot market. But she soon got the hang of it and was pleasantly surprised to find she even began to enjoy the work.

"I would have never even looked for a position like this," Kay said. "Number one, if I had seen it advertised in the paper—I knew nothing about art—I would have never inquired about the position. It has broadened my knowledge and broadened my experiences. I talk with people all over the country. I quote prices on prints, I sell prints every week, and I really enjoy it. I get to talk to all kinds of wonderful people. It lets me communicate with the outside world. It makes me feel good because I am helping the

owner and his wife be able to expand their business and fulfill their dream of maybe someday having a gallery. So it
really has been beneficial to a lot of people.

"It makes me feel real good that I can do this for my
family. I would have never called or applied for this job in a
million years. Even if I would have stumbled onto an ad, I
would have read it and said, 'I can't do this. I don't know
anything about art. I am not capable of fulfilling those
requirements.' That makes you feel good because you find
out that you can do something you didn't think you could
do."

In the process Kay too had managed to put the past
behind her.

THE WAVE OF CHANGE

he negatives of joblessness are easy to see. Besides the obvious loss of income, there may be other losses: sometimes the loss of a standard of living, loss of self-esteem, even loss of a home or a mate. The divorce rate, according to several studies, is as much as 50 percent higher than the national average in families where one earner, usually the man, has lost a job and cannot quickly find an equivalent one, according to the *New York Times*.[1]

Truly, losing a job can ruin at least your day—maybe your year, maybe your life. Not so apparent are the gains. It takes special vision to see the benefits of job loss, but it can be done. Not all jobs are good for the soul; job loss does often lead to something much better down the road; there are ways to recover from the grief that accompanies job loss.

One afternoon I shared a seat on a bus with a woman whose job was to find new words for Webster's *New World Dictionary*. More accurately, the object was *neologisms*, which includes not just new words, but also new meanings for old words and compounds of old words used in new ways. Computer technology has given rise to many of these—e.g., network, reboot, mainframe, multimedia, software, database. This woman said the business world, because of upheaval in the workplace, also has been a fertile field for neologisms—downsizing, outsourcing, telecommuting, reengineering.

I was pleased to be able to give her a new one she had not heard that derived from both the computer and business realms—"repurposing." I had heard it from a friend who worked for a local computer retailer and had garnered a national reputation of sorts as an expert communicator on the subject of digital video, a mushrooming field that may someday be as familiar to the average consumer as microwaves and fax machines. One day he informed me that he had been "repurposed." He explained that, just as software designed for one application can be modified and converted to another application, so had he been repurposed from working with this new digital video technology to selling service contracts to computer customers.

This was not a happy occasion. He spent the weekend in bed, immobilized by depression. Months later, he was still working in the same place, tormented by the desire to leave, but kept in check by the fear of risking the little that he still had to find something better, as well as the remote possibility that things would someday return to normal at his current job. I almost wished that he would be fired, as I had been, so he could get on with life.

WORKAHOLICS AND CODEPENDENTS

There's another neologism of the 1990s: "job lock." Usually, it refers to the immobilization related to the fear of losing employment benefits—especially health insurance, which is expensive under any circumstances, but for some people with medical problems cannot be purchased at any price. But the term could be useful for situations such as my computer friend's, in which a life becomes totally dependent upon a job that has become a veritable puppet master. There are thousands of people like this, probably millions. It's a sickness that has become endemic to entire organizations themselves, according to Anne Wilson Schaef and Diane Fassel, authors of *The Addictive Organization*. They define an addiction as anything we feel we have to lie about and that we're not willing to give up to make our lives fuller and healthier. It's surely no accident that America's most socially acceptable addiction has nothing to do with pills or booze. It's called "workaholism."

Everyone knows the familiar scenario of the family torn apart by an alcoholic or substance abuser whose erratic, even destructive, behavior keeps other members of the family in a constant terrorized state. It's the scenario that has given rise to another neologism—codependency. Simply put, people who subordinate their own feelings and needs in order to control the behavior of an alcoholic, for example, in a very real sense also share the alcoholic's addiction; they are codependent.

But by the same token, how many would recognize the same pattern in the workplace? Schaef and Fassel say these real-life scenarios are identical to the patterns observed in ACOAs—adult children of alcoholics. In *The Addictive Organization*, one woman described a father who was completely consumed by his work:

> We rarely saw him. Sometimes he stayed in the city overnight or on big projects he would be gone for weeks at a time. Work was the overriding excuse for everything, family celebrations, plans and vacations all bowed to the demands of work. We could never count on anything. My father married his work and it had the excitement of a mistress. I don't think my mother or our family were ever second place in my father's life, I believe for him we didn't

exist at all. I grew up spending inordinate amounts of time thinking about my father, yet never really knowing him. I hate him for this and I miss him deeply.[2]

There may be inner reasons for that kind of behavior that go back to family relationship dynamics. The workplace—dysfunctional as it may be—can represent a refuge for the workaholic, who is better at work than he is at relationships. The addiction is subtle, but strong. Our boss may become a surrogate parent, according to Schaef and Fassel, to fulfill needs that were never met at home—attention, encouragement, approval. Denial comes in when we hide from ourselves the truth that, just as with the false promise of drugs, we will never be able to get what we want in the end. Nevertheless, we maintain the fiction that fulfillment lies just around the corner, if we only work a little harder, a little longer. And when we fail, we at least look heroic to others—a hard worker, maybe even a martyr.

It's a scary thought that in many organizations the "best" employees often come from the most dysfunctional homes. These are the ones, according to Schaef and Fassel, who are willing to subordinate their own needs and "let the company become their family." Thus, they are willing to do whatever it takes—longer hours, more responsibilities— just to maintain acceptance by the organization. No burden is too heavy; no sacrifice is too great. The rest of us, out of economic necessity, may find ourselves forced to play along and get sucked into the same dynamics. We've become codependent.

It's scary for a couple of reasons. At root, this hold on people's lives—unquestioning attachment to an organization that defines our very identity—is little different from the dynamics of Jonestown, Waco's Branch Davidians, and other cults, though the outward goals may be more benign or, at least, less controversial. The other scary question is, What happens when the organization revokes your membership and says, "Your services are no longer required"?

No wonder people are devastated by layoffs/firings—some much more than others. The psychic blow can be crushing when it threatens the core of their being.

David Noer, in *Healing the Wounds,* wrote: "People who are organizationally codependent have enabled the system to control their sense of worth and self-esteem at the same time that they invest tremendous energy attempting to control the system. . . . If who you are is where you work, what are you if you lose your job?"[3]

SICK SURVIVORS

Or, for that matter, who are you when other heads start rolling and yours is spared from the chopping block? Not necessarily that much better off. That's why Noer coined the term *layoff survivor sickness* for those left behind but definitely not unaffected.

"Words commonly used to describe the symptoms of layoff survivor sickness," wrote Noer, "are *anger, depression, fear, distrust,* and *guilt.* People with survivor sickness have often been described as having a reduced desire to take risks, a lowered commitment to the job, and a lack of spontaneity."[4]

As either a victim or survivor, there's anger and shame that can be destructive if acted out or turned inward and allowed to harden into bitterness and resentment. The results can be incapacitating at a time when initiative, energy, and resilience are needed the most. But that's exactly what happens when those feelings get stuffed, which is often the strategy of choice among people who want to show the world a stiff upper lip. Like junior Cal Ripken, Jrs., it's more socially acceptable to keep playing with pain.

Why should layoff/firing survivors suffer similar repercussions as the victims? It seems to defy common sense. Some counselors refer to this process in terms of the Lifegiver Principle, in which the Lifegiver can be a parent, an employer, or some other figure of significance who can impact our well-being, such as a spouse in a codependent relationship. An analogy would be to the family in divorce whose children struggle with feelings of guilt, as if they had been somehow responsible for the marital split. *The Lifegiver cannot be wrong; so it must be me*, goes the reasoning. Similarly, says Noer, "There is a sense that you have done something wrong if you get laid off."[5]

The problem with internalizing—stuffing feelings—is they don't just disappear; they fester under cover. King Solomon said three thousand years ago, "A cheerful heart is good medicine, but a crushed spirit dries up the bones" (Proverbs 17:22). That's where people of faith have a leg up on others, if they have another source of life from which to draw—the ultimate Lifegiver—so the loss of a job does not mean loss of identity, meaning, and self-worth. Unemployment is not a total loss if out of it comes a new experience in self-knowledge or even a spiritual awakening, as often happens to a person after the death of a loved one.

For me, it took an employment crisis—and the resulting feelings of despair and depression—to realize that I had a problem with my priorities. In the scheme of things—God, family, job—I had unwittingly elevated my career out of reasonable proportion. Solomon, I think, would have called it idolatry.

GRIEVING YOUR LOSSES

Part of reinventing your career is to bring closure to the anger, fear, and grief you feel. The crushed spirit must be attended to, even if it means allowing the untidiness of spilled emotions. That may mean crying or even raging—for a season. That may seem awkward or unnatural, but if you're frozen in inactivity or despair, that's a sure sign of unfinished emotional business. King Solomon said there is a time for everything, including "a time to weep and a time to laugh, a time to mourn and a time to dance" (Ecclesiastes 3:4). Release also can involve talking things through with a trusted partner, friend, spouse, or support group. If you have none of the above, that in itself is a problem that needs to be addressed. Your network is too small—or too shallow.

The words of Baltasar Gracián, the seventeenth-century Spanish Jesuit savant, are still apropos more than three hundred years later:

> There is gratification in sharing joyful events and an advantage to partnership. More important is to discover someone to help shoulder your misfortunes. The hour of danger, the shadow of distress, will seem less forbidding with someone at your side. . . . This explains why the intelligent physician, having missed the cure, does not miss calling another, who under the name of consultant helps him carry the coffin. Divide with another your burdens and your sorrows. For misfortune, always difficult, is doubly unbearable to him who stands alone.[6]

We live in an age when many people gnash their teeth at the promotions, raises, and other successes of their associates or even take secret pleasure in their misfortune—what the Germans call *Schadenfreude*. But the apostle Paul set a higher standard: "Rejoice with those who rejoice; mourn with those who mourn" (Romans 12:15). That is the kind of friend you need, someone who can share your pain. Paul calls God Himself "the Father of compassion and the God of all comfort, who comforts us in all our troubles, so that we can comfort those in any trouble with the comfort we ourselves have received from God" (2 Corinthians 1:3–4). Notice how the comforting process makes us partakers of the divine.

But the greatest resistance to breaking the emotional logjam may come from within. Thomas Gordon, an expert in organizational psychology, says that from our earliest years we are conditioned to regard feelings almost as dangerous enemies. This attitude is embedded in numerous messages: "Don't feel bad. . . . Swallow your pride. . . . Hold your temper. . . . Bite your tongue." In *Leadership Effectiveness Training*, Gordon wrote two decades ago that there is a "strong ban" in the workplace to such feelings as irritation, anger, frustration, disappointment, hurt, fear, futility, despair, hate, bitterness, and discouragement. There is little reason to doubt that such tendencies would carry over into unemployment.

"While *experiencing* such feelings is not unhealthy, *repressing* them is," according to Gordon. "Continually bottling up your feelings is very definitely 'hazardous to your health' and can ultimately cause ulcers, headaches, heartburn, high blood pressure, spastic colon, or any number of other psychosomatic problems. Repressed feelings can also reduce your effectiveness just by distracting you from your work."[7]

And if you are out of a job, your work is finding a job—or reinventing your career.

Cliff Hakim, a career consultant, recommends an exercise called storytelling that can have both immediate and long-term benefits. Catharsis—giving vent to negative emotions—and the closure that comes from sharing the account of your career trials and tribulations can bring welcome relief to the soul. It can also help regroup your forces for a new game on life's chessboard. Storytelling, according to Hakim in *When You Lose Your Job*, involves "talking with people who will listen, not offer judgments, about your loss, fears, and abilities. By telling your story, you'll have the opportunity to share your feelings, then name them. Second, you can filter out what you do and don't want to share with a potential employer."[8]

It's important to develop a "no sour grapes" explanation of your job loss, which should be part of this exercise. Rick Crow of the Cuyahoga County Reemployment Services Center said few things turn off prospective employers faster than sour grapes. "The employer doesn't want to think you have some unfinished business that you might finish with him," he said.

Above all, lay the facts to rest and face the truth fully. Noer says many struggling employees have to face the fact that they may be "acting out a play that closed long ago." Denial must stop. Employment insecurity may not be a temporary situation; it may become a way of life. There may be more than one job loss in the average worker's future. Reality, unpalatable as it can be, must be faced.[9]

RIDING THE EMOTIONAL ROLLER COASTER

At the Cuyahoga County Reemployment Services Center, the average job seeker has been out of work for six months. In Ohio, that's the total duration of unemployment compensation. So by this time things are getting very serious. Some of these people have been going through the motions without much progress. Some have been paralyzed by inaction. Many of them have unfinished business. Oftentimes, they haven't grieved their loss yet.

Robert E. Paponetti, center director, said there's a correlation with the classic grief process in studies of death and dying. But not everybody is ready to accept the idea right away. Some, even job placement workers, tend to regard the concept as a little too much like pop psychology. Until, that is, they see it for themselves directly.

"When the program was first set up," said Paponetti, "this piece was in there and some of our job developers, who are on the back end, who are really working hard to get jobs, they kind of scoffed at this whole emotional part— 'That's touchy-feely, it's just slowing down the whole process.' So, I said, let's try to circumvent that. We will identify people who the day they come in, if they feel like they're ready and we think they are ready, we will have them go right into the next process, Learning How to Get a Job, which we tried for a couple weeks.

"What was happening, our instructors who were teaching the employability stuff said, 'You know, we are spending more time talking about the actual job of looking for a job. They need to go back and get this piece. They have to go back and talk about it and vent and bring it to a closure.'"

Rick Crow handles this issue by walking counselees through a graphical roller coaster, "The Wave of Change," modeled on the grief process. Then they talk about their feelings in small groups. Crow said people who have been unable to open up to anyone else, including close family members, find it natural, if not easy, to do so among others who have had the same experience. And, in doing so, they find some release, especially from the feeling of isolation, that "I'm the only one in this boat."

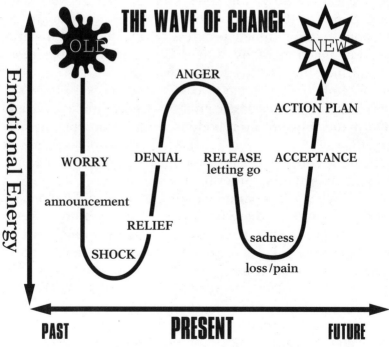

Courtesy of Cuyahoga County Reemployment Services Center

In the typical layoff/firing scenario, the emotional roller coaster starts with *worry*, as rumors swirl that an ax is about to fall. It is followed by *shock*, with the actual announcement of jobs being cut, a letdown in terms of emotional energy. Ironically, the next reaction is *relief*, as the fear of the unknown is dispelled by naked reality. Everyone now knows who must take the long walk off the short plank. That particular anxiety is over. The devil that we know is preferable to the one we don't know.

Next on the roller-coaster ride comes *denial*, as the mind throws up defenses against the external threat to its security. *"No!"* it cries. "It can't be. There must be some mistake." The next reaction is *anger*, as reality sinks in and the sense of outrage against the violation builds. But anger cannot sustain itself forever, and eventually there is a *release*, as the emotion spends itself and the person begins to let go, through exhaustion if nothing else. In emotional terms, this is the second trough as the wave of loss and pain overwhelms us.

At last, there is another upswing that puts the wave of change behind us, as we reach an *acceptance* of the unchangeable circumstance and begin to put it behind us. This is the point where we develop our *action plan* for getting on with the rest of our life. That might mean snapping out of the defeat mode, updating the résumé, and starting to knock on doors. Or it might mean just the opposite— hanging up the job search and going into business for oneself.

Whatever the case, the time for pity parties is over; the time for action has come.

NOTES

1. "The Downsizing of America," *New York Times*, series, March 3 to March 9, 1996.
2. Anne Wilson Schaef and Diane Fassel, *The Addictive Organization:*

Why We Overwork, Cover Up, Pick Up the Pieces, Please the Boss, and Perpetuate Sick Organizations (New York: Harper & Row, 1988), 132.

3. David M. Noer, *Healing the Wounds: Overcoming the Trauma of Layoffs and Revitalizing Downsized Organizations* (San Francisco: Jossey-Bass, 1993), 136, 141.

4. Ibid., 13.

5. Ibid., 52.

6. J. Leonard Kaye and Julie Rubenstein, eds., *The Wisdom of Baltasar Gracián: A Practical Manual for Good and Perilous Times* (New York: Pocket, 1992), 17.

7. Thomas Gordon, *Leadership Effectiveness Training* (New York: Wyden, 1977), 75.

8. Cliff Hakim, *When You Lose Your Job: Laid Off, Fired, Early Retired, Relocated, Demoted, Unchallenged* (San Francisco: Berrett-Koehler, 1993), 36, 187.

9. Noer, *Healing the Wounds*, 143.

5 AT THE CORE

ow does the jobless person manage—let alone master—the change that's been forced upon him?

Ironically, much of the answer may be found within the very organizations that have been generating all of this joblessness in the first place. Faced with challenges to their very survival in a world of global competition and rapid technological change, business organizations have been forced to reinvent themselves in a couple of key ways—*discovering a sense of purpose or mission* and *focusing on their core competencies*. Individuals will have to do much the same thing to reinvent their own careers and survive the threats to their economic survival.

DISCOVERING PURPOSE

David Noer's prescription is detachment—letting go—and connecting to a *core purpose:* "Each person must determine his or her unique purpose in life."[1] If this language sounds familiar, it's much the same talk emanating from the executive suites these days in regard to the large organization. Now everybody is writing mission statements, vision statements, and statements of purpose.

The late W. Edwards Deming, a main pillar of the quality movement through his Total Quality Management system, brought the organizational mission to the forefront of attention in the world of business management. Significantly, the very first of his fourteen famous TQM principles exhorts organizations to create "constancy of purpose" for products and services. This is trickier than it sounds; it requires raising the sights and taking the long view.

At the turn of the last century there were two very different buggy whip makers. The first one committed itself to making the best buggy whips on the market. The second one devoted itself to transportation. Today, the first one is history. The second one is making automotive carburetors.

A number of automakers in the early 1900s started out as bicycle companies that were willing to reinvent themselves. Remember Motorola? It purposed to create a superior, repairable product, but it lost its TV market to foreign competitors who could make superior products that didn't need repair. Whether it's a buggy whip company, a bicycle maker, an automaker, or an electronics manufacturer, the principle is the same: It not only has to invent new products and services, it has to reinvent itself.

The same is true for individuals. If you don't know where you're headed, someone said, you may end up where you don't want to be. Images abound: the gasping pilgrim clawing his way to a Himalayan summit in anxious search of truths about the meaning of life; the sidewalk derelict huddled over a steam heat grate, devoid of any direction in life; the business professional climbing the career ladder, only to find it's leaning against the wrong building.

As King Solomon once said: "The purposes of a man's heart are deep waters, but a man of understanding draws them out" (Proverbs 20:5).

Counselors, therapists, and others who study human behavior have identified several major common denominators as core personal needs. The classic one in Psychology 101 texts is Abraham Maslow's hierarchy of needs. Higher up the ladder after the basic physiological needs (food, shelter, and so on) and physical safety are the more interpersonal drives—acceptance, esteem, and self-actualization. Other authors have expressed similar principles in slightly different terms, such as relationship, integrity, and impact.

Relationship involves our social needs, which include being affirmed as a person with worth and dignity as a valued member of a larger whole, even if it's only a partnership of two. *Integrity* relates to issues of fairness, justice, honesty, and the need for equitable and forthright treatment in school, work, politics, or any other organization, no matter the size. For managers, the issues will involve the credibility of their leadership in terms of practicing what they preach.

Impact is sometimes called significant purpose. It involves making a contribution, making a difference, standing at the plate and getting a hit. In *Understanding People*, psychologist Lawrence J. Crabb, Jr., defines impact as "a desire to be adequate for a meaningful task, a desire to know that we are capable of taking hold of our world and doing something valuable and well."[2]

The first time I ever saw a battery-powered hand drill was at least twenty years ago in one of the Old Man's Cave parks in southern Ohio. It was in the hands of a man intent on inscribing his name upon a boulder located on a scenic overlook. Outraged, my wife sought out a park ranger after we returned to our camp. The ranger assured her that the problem had already been dealt with. Some young "hippie" types, similarly outraged, had come upon the man and made a citizen's arrest. "But people would be able to read *my name* for a hundred years!" the man reportedly exclaimed as he was served his citation.

Our misguided Michelangelo illustrated dramatically, if in a less than socially acceptable manner, that the desire for impact on our world is a deep, primal need. Is there any question how directly impact applies to the workplace? "We want to know that we are capable of doing a job that needs to be done," wrote Crabb. "We want to leave a mark on our world, a real and enduring difference that matters."[3]

If impact—or significant purpose—is such a driving force, why wouldn't an individual as much as a big corporation need a personal statement of purpose? Perry Pascarella and Mark A. Frohman have described in *The Purpose-Driven Organization* the corporate benefits such an exercise provides—direction, focus, policy, meaning, challenge, and passion. "All of us want to be more than a number at work," they wrote. "We want our work to enhance our self-respect and satisfy our desire to achieve. In short, we want our work to provide meaning for us. A purpose statement provides meaning by defining something greater to relate to than the job itself. It offers a broader context in which to fit our daily work."[4]

Purpose is even more applicable to the jobless individual looking to get back into the race. James Collins and Jerry Porras, authors of *Built to Last: Successful Habits of Visionary Companies,* describe purpose as a "guiding star" to reestablish direction and a reason for organizational (or personal) existence. It gives meaning to work and something to believe in. Lack of a clear overall aim was a major downfall, for example, of U.S. strategy in Vietnam.

FOCUSING ON THE CORE

Before addressing the *personal* statement of purpose, it would be well to consider some further dimensions of organizational mission. In their six-year study of long-lasting, visionary companies, Collins and Porras focused on what they called "core ideology," which consists of *core values* plus *purpose.* Core values comprise the organization's basic tenets and guiding principles. Purpose is defined as "the organization's fundamental reasons for existence beyond just making money."[5]

A poor purpose statement for Walt Disney, for example, would have been "We exist to make cartoons for kids," having little power to motivate anyone for very long, according to Collins and Porras. Fortunately, Disney did better than that: "To bring happiness to millions" and to celebrate, nurture, and promulgate "wholesome American values." These values include fanatical attention to consistency and detail and continuous progress via creativity, dreams, and imagination.[6]

Motorola again provides a good example. Collins and Porras said the electronics giant was able to evolve from

> battery eliminators for home radios, to car radios, to home television, to semiconductors, to integrated circuits, to cellular communications, to satellite systems, and to who-knows-what in the twenty-first century—yet never outgrow its fundamental quest "to honorably serve the community by providing products and services of superior quality at a fair price."[7]

Among its values are continuous self-renewal, tapping the "latent creative power within us," and "treating employees with dignity, and honesty, integrity, and ethics in all aspects of business."[8]

Sometimes values are expressed in terms of *vision*, and some organizations craft both a mission and a vision statement. One such organization is America's tenth largest employer, Columbia/HCA Healthcare Corp., the largest hospital organization in the country. Its mission: "To work with our employees, physicians, and volunteers to provide a continuum of quality healthcare cost-effectively for the people in the communities we serve." Its vision: "To work with employees and physicians to build a company that is focused on the well-being of people, that is patient oriented, that offers the most advanced technology and information systems, that is financially sound, and that is synonymous with quality, cost-effective healthcare."

America's hospitals provide vivid examples of one of the forces behind the "flattening" of organizations and the loss of jobs—outsourcing. Historically, hospitals as community institutions have tried to be full-service operations with their own employees staffing a wide range of departments from laundry to food service to power plants to information systems. This self-sufficiency has all but ended in recent years as financial pressures have forced hospitals to reduce head counts, focus on what they can do best, and farm out the rest to other organizations that could provide those services with greater quality and economy. Hospitals found themselves forced to narrow their focus to their *core competencies*—direct health care services. Groundskeeping, housekeeping, and security are more properly the core competencies of landscape, cleaning, and security firms.

This is the same thing the public sector has been discovering in governmental operations down to the level of townships that farm out trash hauling. There it's called "privatizing." But it's the same difference—contracting out to those who are the best and most efficient providers of those services. And it's the same principle employed by commercial enterprises in a form called "niche marketing," in which a specialty food company, for example, might specialize in imported fish from South America because it has found a very specific place in the market where it can excel and dominate.

And increasingly, individuals must do much the same thing in their own personal careers.

PERSONAL STATEMENT OF PURPOSE

Some of the best advice I got when I decided to try self-employment was to narrow my focus in terms of the services I would offer to the public. I called my one-man band Adams Business Communications (ABC). I knew I would be offering writing, editing, and public relations services, but I also considered adding videography to the portfolio. With an eye to the future, I hoped to diversify my communications offerings beyond the printed word.

But Tony, a church friend and chief financial officer for a large company, asked a few challenging questions. Did I have experience with video? Was I particularly technically minded? No, I had to answer in each case. My core competencies were really writing, editing, and public relations. Then, said Tony, stick with those and even narrow them further to a niche you can dominate by being the best in that area so that people will think of you when they think of that service. If you want to work in the video area, find a good specialist and form a strategic alliance, he said.

I soon discovered the wisdom of that approach. Through my network of contacts after sixteen years in the same city, I was able to find opportunities as an independent contractor helping out PR agencies with special projects and as a freelance business writer. The fact that I had published a couple of novels helped convince me—my core competency was writing, especially on business topics and health care. I decided to make that my stock-in-trade and came up with a slogan that I put on my business cards: *Ideas on Paper, Words in Print.*

A number of observations began to jell in my mind. I began to realize that I really worked best on my own rather than as part of a team or under an authoritarian structure. I was strongly self-directed and actually enjoyed intensely creative projects under my own management. The words of my late father, a small businessman, when we had once discussed my journalism career came back to me: "Well, Son, nobody gets rich working for somebody else." At the time, the words had meant little to me because I was more of an idealist than a materialist. "Getting rich" to me was about as attractive an idea as getting old.

But now I realized that it didn't necessarily have to

mean having a lot of money. For me, a "rich" life might be simply having economic independence, maybe finding out if I could run my own business. When I really thought about it, I'd always disliked being an employee. I had no aversion to work, but having to report five days a week at prescribed hours to a specific place to receive instructions felt all too much like indentured servitude. But I had never given these feelings much thought. If I had, I probably would have figured this was simply the way things were and I was wrong to feel that way.

My statement of purpose, had I actually written it out at that point, would have been something like this: *I am committed to working as an independent contractor on projects of my choosing involving ideas on paper and words in print. As a writer and editor, I value the self-direction, independence, and creative satisfaction of the writing process itself. I am not a natural organization-climber nor administrator; my role within an organization would more naturally be as a teacher, trainer, or communicator.*

Here is a fine but important point. It was not that I couldn't function as a supervisor. In fact, I had worked as an assistant city editor of a large metropolitan newspaper for a number of years, supervising reporters. But was that my core competency? Probably not. I could do it adequately, but never as effectively as I could do the work of a writer. The reality is that in today's competitive times neither organizations nor individuals can afford to play anything but their strongest suit. How many people are getting stressed out and burned out trying to play roles that are not genuinely their own? Too many, no doubt.

Confusion here can be fatal. Without understanding your core competencies, it is even harder to identify your life mission, vision, and purpose. In the church, we say if you want to know God's plan for your life, look at your gifts—another way of saying core competencies. If you don't have a gift for public speaking and don't like working with people, for example, it's not likely you're being called to the ministry.

It also needs to be *your* mission and vision, not someone else's expectations. As an early member of the baby boom generation, I was one of the square pegs that tried to fit into the round holes of science and technology in the wake of the Sputnik challenge. There was a rampant fear in the late 1950s and early 1960s that the United States would lose out to the Soviets in the technology race unless America mounted a crash effort among its schoolchildren to produce more scientists and technicians by directing them into advanced science and math programs. It took me a few years in college to unlearn this programming and, through personal failures, to discover that my real gifts were in an entirely different area.

Finding a niche first involves self-knowledge, knowing your gifts. The principle has many and varied applications, even for *Reinventing Your Career*. While this book deals with some of the practical steps involved in the job search process, it is not intended to reinvent the wheel. There are many good books on the market that address that issue thoroughly. Nor does *Reinventing Your Career* directly address the ethical/moral/political questions of the layoff/firing phenomenon so much as it discusses personal ramifications. This book's niche is more in terms of careers than jobs, more for long-term personal self-discovery than for immediate contemporary social problems. Its success will be determined largely by how well it fills that role.

☞ **What about you? Do you know what your real gifts are? If you were to write your own personal mission statement, what would it say?**

NOTES

1. David M. Noer, *Healing the Wounds: Overcoming the Trauma of Lay-*

offs and Revitalizing Downsized Organizations (San Francisco: Jossey-Bass, 1993), 151.

2. Lawrence J. Crabb, Jr., *Understanding People: Deep Longings for Relationship* (Grand Rapids: Zondervan, 1987), 114.
3. Ibid., 113.
4. Perry Pascarella and Mark A. Frohman, *The Purpose-Driven Organization: Unleashing the Power of Direction and Commitment* (San Francisco: Jossey-Bass, 1989), 35.
5. James C. Collins and Jerry I. Porras, *Built to Last: Successful Habits of Visionary Companies* (New York: HarperBusiness, 1994), 73.
6. Ibid., 70–71.
7. Ibid., 77.
8. Ibid., 70.

6

THE JOURNEY OF SELF-DISCOVERY

What is a career? *Webster's New World Dictionary* defines it as "one's progress through life in a particular vocation." The word originally meant a race course. In fact, the word "car" is a linguistic relative. The verb "to career" means "to move at full speed; to rush wildly," according to *Webster's*. In addition to the idea of a race there is something else: There is an assumption that the natural state is one vocation—literally, "calling"—per person. For life.

As we have seen, however, those days are gone, perhaps forever. No more than we would expect to drive the same car all our lives can we expect lifetime employment or even a lifetime career. The marketplace is changing too rapidly. In that case, what good are all our talents and gifts, innately fixed as they are?

A 1996 report of the President's Council of Economic Advisors said the U.S. economy was actually producing *more* jobs than were being lost through downsizing—and most of the new ones were well paying—but that worker anxieties were due to the *speed of transformation*" in the constantly changing labor market. In other words, it wasn't that unemployment was increasing, but that it was becoming increasingly a game of musical jobs at an accelerating tempo. The odds were strongly in favor of finding another situation, as long as you showed a little hustle.

The worker of the 1990s has to feel somewhat like the character Bink in Piers Anthony's novels set in the amusing and pun-filled fantasy world called Xanth, where every citizen was expected to demonstrate a magical gift by adulthood. Unfortunately, Bink couldn't identify his gift, if he had one.

"Yet how many talents really did help their people?" a frustrated Bink wondered. "One person could make a leaf of a tree wither and die as he looked at it. Another could create the odor of sour milk. Another could make insane laughter bubble up from the ground. These were all magic, no question about it—but what use were they? Why should such people qualify as citizens of Xanth while Bink, who was smart, strong, and handsome, was disqualified? Yet that was the absolute rule: no nonmagical person could remain beyond his quarter-century mark."[1]

Without spoiling the delightful story for anyone, suffice it to say that Bink's journey of self-discovery has a happy outcome. As I have considered the different people I know with their different gifts, I am sometimes reminded of the kingdom of Xanth. We, too—in the land that the inhabitants of Xanth call *Mundania*—are all unique individuals and often have to engage in a bit of self-discovery as our own gifts may be very different from those of others around us. Sometimes I am tempted to disparage my own repertoire. I long to wield powerful magic—exert *significant impact* on my world—when my real gifts may seem more akin to creating the odor of sour milk or laughter bubbling from the ground.

Thirty years ago in college, I had a part-time job in the university's Office Services department, operating an Addressograph machine. This was the low-tech device with trays of metal plates that was once used to stamp names and addresses on outgoing materials to an organization's mailing list, in this case alumni and financial supporters. Considering what happened to that technology in subsequent years, it was good that I continued my studies. It was not to be a skill I could ever fall back on. Today, Addressograph operators have about as much calling as keypunchers or Linotypists in the era of modern computers and electronic cold-type printing.

Not that those people were put permanently out of work. Many keypunch operators have made the leap into newer computer technologies and programming, while many Linotype operators now can be found with a glue gun or razor knife in hand in the newspaper or magazine's layout department. Today, when jobs and job descriptions change faster than Paris fashions, career counselors speak in terms of *transferable skills*. For machine operators forced to change horses in midcareer, transferable skills might include an interest in operating precision equipment, good hand-eye coordination and mechanical ability, and a tolerance for long periods of performing routine tasks repetitively.

Transferable skills are different from *job content* skills, which are the more obvious skills peculiar to a specific job, such as measuring, cutting, and hammering for a carpenter and typing and taking dictation for a secretary. As the name implies, transferable skills can be transferred from one job—or one career—to another, such as instructing others, managing money, managing people, meeting deadlines, meeting with the public, negotiating, organizing/managing projects, public speaking, and written communications skills. Other transferable skills, based on a listing from the Cuyahoga County Reemployment Services Center:

- **Dealing with things**—assembling, building, constructing, repairing, driving, manual tasks, inspecting, operating.
- **Dealing with data**—checking, classifying, comparing, compiling, counting, evaluating, investigating, recording, locating, observing, researching, synthesizing, taking inventory.
- **Working with people**—administering, caring, confronting, counseling, demonstrating, mediating.
- **Leadership**—arranging, competing, deciding, delegating, directing, explaining, influencing, initiating, managing, motivating, negotiating, planning, running, solving.
- **Creative/Artistic**—creating, moving/dancing, drawing, expressing, performing, acting, presenting, designing, composing.

In my case, the moves from journalism to public relations and then to freelance business communications required no special retraining because of the transferable skills common to all three—interviewing, researching, writing, editing, typing, word processing, and so on. Career experts break down such areas into even finer sets, such as the use of logic, analyzing, comprehending, interpreting, verbalizing, influencing, and forming conclusions. Rick Crow of the Cuyahoga County Reemployment Services Center tells counselees that most people have no idea how many skills they have. If you include learned behaviors all the way down to tying your shoes, experts have counted somewhere around 10,000 average "skills," he says.

In *When You Lose Your Job,* Cliff Hakim advocates taking stock of things in terms of a "career theme," which he defines as

> words, phrases, and feelings that have repeated throughout your career. For example, "helping others," "develop-

ing new ideas," or "making better what someone else has started." Think of it as a melody you've played—in the jobs you've had, in the projects you've completed, and in the roles you've assumed, both professionally and personally.[2]

☞ Take a few minutes and make a personal inventory of your skills. Then keep the list as a future reference for considering how they may transfer to other employment, even a different career.

GETTING THE DATA

Each of us as a whole person, of course, is much more than our isolated skill sets. William Bridges *(JobShift)* recommends a DATA search—identifying your Desires, Abilities, Temperaments, and Assets. He couches *Abilities* in the form of the question, "What are you really good at?" These are the skills and talents—personal *core competencies*—that we have been considering. In their purest sense, these are our more general aptitudes—like mechanical or musical gifts—as opposed to the more developed proficiencies we normally think of as specific skills, such as drywall hanging or piano tuning.[3]

Temperament refers to our individual preferences and values that define our working and learning style, in which one environment is acceptable while another would be unsuitable or even frustrating. Such temperaments may be expressed in terms of a continuum, such as independence versus conformity, as measured by instruments like the Career Orientation Placement and Evaluation Survey (COPES)™. An independent type, for example, might work better as a freelancer than would a conformist, who is by nature more of a team player under supervision.

Other such work values include investigative vs. accepting; practical vs. carefree; leadership vs. supportive; orderliness vs. noncompulsive; recognition vs. privacy; aesthetic vs. realistic; social vs. self-concern. "Investigative," for example, describes the person who is intellectually curious and thrives on solving complex tasks. Other widely used systems include the Myers-Briggs Type Inventory (MBTI), which assesses temperaments according to sixteen types, and the Self-Directed Search (SDS), which helps match interests and abilities with specified career fields. Inventories like the COPES, MBTI, and SDS are useful tools for self-evaluation, although they require some interpretation and may be accessed through career counselors, who are generally listed in telephone directories under Career and Vocational Counselors.

By taking the COPES at the Cuyahoga County Reemployment Services Center, I verified that my work as a freelance writer was not just a situation by default, but was in line with my work values—my three highest being Investigative (intellectual curiosity), Aesthetic (artistic appreciation), and Independence. This was further confirmed by two other inventories, called the Career Ability Placement Survey (CAPS)™, and the Career Occupational Preference System (COPS-P)™, which showed both ability and interest in the areas of written and oral communications.

Job seekers taking the CAPS test are measured in eight primary areas—mechanical reasoning, spatial relations, verbal reasoning, numerical ability, language usage, word knowledge, perceptual speed and accuracy, and manual speed and dexterity. Those, of course, relate back to *Abilities*. These are different from our last "A" in DATA, *Assets*.

Assets are the relative advantages we may enjoy over others, all other things being equal, such as innate gifts and abilities. Although an ability or even one's temperament may be an asset, we are speaking primarily of the competitive advantages that come from experience. It may be having studied French or Spanish. It may be a network of contacts of people who can help by providing information or opening doors that are shut to others.

That leaves the area of interests—or the first letter in DATA, "D" for *Desires*. In terms of careers, the COPS-P groups them in eight major clusters: Science—medical/life and physical. Technology—electrical, mechanical, civil. Outdoor—nature and agribusiness. Business—finance and management. Computation. Communication—written and oral. Arts—performing and design. Service—instructional and social. For further information, you may want to consult the *Dictionary of Occupational Titles*. There is not much ground left uncovered by this system. Someone bitten by the bug to become a ski instructor, for example, may be surprised to find himself listed under "Arts, Entertaining-Performing" DOT #153.227-018.

We are not referring here, however, to career decisions driven so much by things such as pay or benefits or status, but by, as some have put it, what makes our "toes tingle." It may be a radical idea to some, but it's about what we enjoy doing, the things that bring us personal fulfillment in their performance. Bridges suggests that some of the questions we may want to ask ourselves to identify these desires include: What do I want (open-ended)? What do I want to be doing and how do I want to be living in ten years? What was I meant to accomplish with my life?[4]

In other words, what would it take to bring a little magic here to Mundania?

"Character" Skills

There are other skills that we seldom think of because they're almost too familiar; we use them every day to survive and make life work. They are called "adaptive skills" because they allow us to adapt or adjust to a variety of situations, including work. They could also be called "good worker traits" because they are especially valued by employers, such as getting to work on time and getting along well with others.

Other adaptive skills:

- **Quality**—productive, assertive, capable, competent, creative, efficient, independent, intelligent, original, persistent, resourceful, practical, strong, tenacious, versatile, well organized.
- **Attitude**—cheerful, accepts supervision, flexible, energetic, eager, enthusiastic, motivated, friendly, good-natured, modest, optimistic, confident.
- **Work ethic**—honest, dependable, reliable, discreet, good attendance, conscientious, helpful, loyal, patient, responsible, sincere, steady, thrifty, trustworthy.

Conversely, there are traits and behaviors that are about as endearing to employers as higher taxes. Absenteeism and tardiness naturally rank high on employer surveys as major reasons for firing an employee. But even higher are negative personal characteristics, including lying, dishonesty, ego problems, arrogance, overconfidence, aggressiveness, lack of dedication or commitment, unconcern, not being a team player, poor attitude, and being a poor listener.

Other characteristics that rub employers wrong include not getting along, poor communicating, whining, complaining, poor attitude toward the company, not utilizing one's full potential, laziness, lack of motivation or enthusiasm. Even poor eye contact, excessive nervousness, lack of creativity, and lack of integrity make the problem list. Poor work habits leading to discharge include not following instructions, not doing the job, lack of productivity, not finishing tasks, "goofing off" and "fooling around," doing personal business on company time, irresponsibility, unreliability, unpredictability, inconsistencies, not following policy or procedures, poor decisions, and incompetence.

It should be apparent by now that the so-called adaptive skills—or lack thereof—add up to much the same thing as character qualities. And how important is character? It may determine our very destiny. Consider the following old saying: "Sow a thought, reap an action. Sow an action, reap a habit. Sow a habit, reap a character. Sow a character, reap a destiny." Or as the German poet Novalis (Friedrich von Hardenberg) put it more succinctly: "Character is destiny." On this, too, King Solomon had words of wisdom: "For as he thinketh in his heart, so is he" (Proverbs 23:7 KJV).

Character is the missing dimension of virtues in the equation of talents, skills, gifts, desires, abilities, temperament, and assets. It is the work ethic and the moral quality of our lives that will endure after we are gone. On the way to our destiny, it is the difference we make in life—and the lives of others.

My pastor, the Reverend Donald D. Schaeffer, of Grace Christian and Missionary Alliance Church in Middleburg Heights, Ohio, tells the story of a carpenter who was given the task of building an entire house unsupervised with only a specified budget and a reasonable deadline. The man, thinking himself clever, built the house with a minimum of effort, cutting corners on quality wherever he could, disregarding even safety considerations. He finished so far ahead of schedule that he spent the next few work days fishing. When he returned to work, the owner of the construction company surprised him with a set of keys: The house that he had been building so haphazardly was a gift—for him. The carpenter, considering the miserable heap he had created, realized too late that he had no one to blame but himself.

Some people who have studied character extensively have come up with some intriguing findings. One of those is the fact that character qualities, like vocational skills, tend to appear in clusters. Again, like other abilities, these qualities can be developed and strengthened through consistent discipline. And these clusters can be used to define entire character types, which relates directly to our journey of self-discovery.

Two different organizations have teamed up in this pioneering area: Kimray, Inc., a manufacturer of oil and gas equipment and controls, serving producers and equipment manufacturers in the petroleum industry, and the Institute of Basic Life Principles (IBLP), headed by Bill Gothard, an evangelical Christian well known for his teaching ministry in huge urban seminars. Tom Hill, Kimray chief operating officer, saw what he thought was great potential business application in IBLP's teachings on character qualities, and the two organizations together spawned a new venture called the Character Training Institute in a former Holiday Inn hotel in Oklahoma City, a few blocks from the bombed-out federal building.

"The more rules you make, the more rules you need," Hill said at one of the Institute's first three-day training programs for businesspeople. "You can't write enough rules." He was teaching the businesspeople that good character is an inward motivation springing from the heart that needs to be cultivated by good managers through praise and recognition. His remarks carried the weight of credibility as he explained what cultivating character had done for his business—including reduced employee absenteeism and improved net income.

In the *Character First* training program, managers learn to identify forty-nine discrete character qualities in employees in seven clusters of seven—such as self-control, respectfulness, diligence, thoroughness, dependability, security, and patience. That particular cluster defines the character type known as the Teacher, with which I instantly identified. The teacher is defined as one who "imparts wisdom, maturity, and skill to others, validates direction, and insures completion."

The point is that these principles are not just for managers. They may be helpful signposts along the self-discovery journey for the displaced worker and job seeker, anyone who needs to reinvent his career. Negative personal traits can be diamonds in the rough. If you struggle with being rigid, harsh, overbearing, judgmental, and miserly, cheer up; you may have the character quality of self-control in a distorted measure. *Character First* sorts through the qualities and their distortions.

The other character types are:

- **Visionary**—sees beyond the immediate situation.
- **Server**—meets the needs of others to help them succeed.
- **Organizer**—directs resources for successful completion of goals.
- **Mediator**– compassionately analyzes merits of competing positions.
- **Idealist**—identifies problems, speaks the truth boldly.
- **Provider**—ensures the best use of available resources.

☞ **Everyone has character, positive or negative. What type are you? You may want to write for further information to The Character Training Institute, 520 West Main Street, Oklahoma City, OK 73102-2220.**

NOTES

1. Piers Anthony, *A Spell for Chameleon* (New York: Ballantine, 1977), 6.
2. Cliff Hakim, *When You Lose Your Job: Laid Off, Fired, Early Retired, Relocated, Demoted, Unchallenged* (San Francisco: Berrett-Koehler, 1993), 182.
3. William Bridges, *JobShift: How to Prosper in a World Without Jobs* (Reading, Mass.: Addison-Wesley, 1994), 77.
4. Ibid., 79–82.

7

GETTING OFF THE DIME

The phone rang, but Jerry knew Phyllis would get it. He was taking a nap on the couch, and there was no particular reason to get up just yet. It wasn't quite nine o'clock, and he still felt yucky from the lingering effects of this most recent cold. He seemed to get a lot of those anymore. He turned over and tried to get back to sleep.

Jerry Davenport had become a real couch potato. In the six months since he had lost his job, he had gained twenty pounds just from inactivity. But he felt he deserved to take it easy after years of beating his brains out in those sweatshops where he used to work until getting cast aside like a piece of refuse.

"Jerry!" called Phyllis. "Get up! It's the woman from the Displaced Worker Center. She wants to know if you can come in at ten."

Jerry raised his drowsy head in irritation. "*Ten?* That's only an hour. Ask her if I can see her tomorrow."

Phyllis gave a little snort of apparent frustration and

returned to the kitchen. Jerry could still hear her from the living room.

"Yes, Ms. Tompkins," she said emphatically. "Jerry will be there at ten. Thank you very much."

Uh-oh. Jerry sensed an incident in the making. This suspicion was instantly confirmed as the floorboards telegraphed Phyllis's determined stride coming through the dining room.

"Jerry!" she barked. "If you don't get up off that couch and act like you're alive, I'm going to give you a cold shower with a bucket."

"Go 'way," Jerry murmured.

Phyllis was insistent. "I am not going away. And you're getting up off that couch and going downtown to that appointment or I'll—"

Jerry propped himself up on one elbow and gave her a challenging look. "Or you'll what?"

Phyllis was biting her lip. "Or I'm taking the kids and leaving you, Jerry. And I mean it!"

With that, she spun on her heel and left the room as quickly as she'd entered. Jerry was nonplussed. This wasn't like Phyllis. Normally she didn't make threats like that. Somehow, Jerry believed she wasn't kidding.

"Nice to meet you, Mr. Davenport," said Juanita Tompkins, the job counselor. "Let's just take a minute and fill out this questionnaire. First, why don't you give me your employment history."

Jerry shrugged. "What do you want to know?"

"The basics—the places you worked, how long, what you did there, what skills were required, what you liked about it."

Jerry took a deep breath and thought back twenty years. He was first a stereotyper in the composing room at the *Daily Slant*, turning out page plates for the press room in the old hot-lead process. He did that for nearly ten years until the newspaper announced that it was converting to a cold-type process that would eliminate stereotyping—and stereotypers. During the transition Jerry took some training and did some apprenticing through the union as a keyliner, but his seniority was not high enough to land a permanent slot when the dust cleared.

So for the next several years he tried a variety of low-paying jobs until he could find something in his field. He worked as a convenience store clerk, painted houses, and served as assistant manager of a video rental store until he landed a full-time position as a keyliner, pasting up pages with a razor knife and wax gun for a magazine published locally for car collectors. Unfortunately, three years into that job the magazine was sold to a larger publisher, who moved the jobs of Jerry and others in his department to Baltimore.

It was back to painting houses for another year until he got a good job in the production department of an entertainment magazine for country music, which was one of his personal interests. But again, misfortune struck. This time it was not an out-of-state merger or acquisition, but another technology advance that left him out in the cold. Ownership purchased a new state-of-the-art production system with pagination and print-on-demand capabilities that eliminated Jerry's entire department in a mouse click.

"And how old are you, Mr. Davenport?" asked Ms. Tompkins when he'd finished his account.

"Forty-two," he said. "Please call me Jerry."

She looked up with a sympathetic expression. "Sure, Jerry. So, were you laid off or let go?"

Jerry lowered his eyes. "Let go. Nobody's getting called back."

"How does that make you feel?"

He looked up in mild surprise. "What? You want to know how I . . . *feel?*"

The woman nodded.

Jerry wasn't sure what to say. "Well, I don't know. I'm OK, I guess."

The woman looked skeptical. "I'm serious. You have feelings, don't you?"

Jerry stiffened. "Yeah, sure. But what's the use? It won't change anything. You just take your lumps and move on."

"*Do* you?"

Something in the way she said it irritated him. "That's right. What do you mean?"

"Well, you've been out of work almost six months. Unemployment compensation is about to run out, and still no job. And your wife says you're a basket case—'no oomph,' I think she said."

Now Jerry was really annoyed. "She said *that?*"

Ms. Tompkins nodded. "Is it true?"

He was beginning to get the picture. "Well, maybe it's not so easy anymore finding a job. Don't you think it's normal to get a little discouraged?"

The woman nodded again. "It's also normal for a spouse to feel frustrated. So, you feel discouraged—'a little.' What's that like?"

Jerry shrugged. "No big deal. It just takes me a little longer to get rolling these days, that's all."

"Why do you think that is?"

"Well, I'm over forty now. Doesn't that mean I should be over the hill or something?"

Ms. Tompkins ignored his feeble attempt at humor. "OK. Being older makes it harder to find a job. That doesn't make you angry?"

Now Jerry was starting to get a little stubborn. "Don't think so. Should it?"

"Maybe. Maybe you are and you don't know it. Maybe there's some guilt there too."

Jerry almost laughed. "What are you, a shrink or something?"

The woman smiled. "I'm a licensed psychologist and

counselor. How is everything at home?"

Jerry felt defensive. "You mean, like with the wife and kids?"

She nodded.

"OK, I guess."

The woman looked skeptical again. "No conflict?"

He caught himself. "Well, I take that back. My wife threatened to leave me if I didn't get it together. I don't know why she's acting like that."

"How does that make you feel?"

"I think she's being unreasonable, that's all. Maybe I just don't get it."

The woman smiled kindly. "Look. I'm not really trying to do a whole counseling session here, but I am trying to show you that you need to open up. I think your wife is trying to get you to do that too. You're shut down, Jerry. You need to deal with it, not stuff it."

It was Jerry's turn to be skeptical. He had the improbable mental image of a boarded-up gas station. "I'm shut down?"

She nodded. "Think about it. Shouldn't you be upset—concerned, at least—that your wife would consider leaving you?"

"I don't know. Maybe. I guess I don't like thinking about it. The last thing I need is . . . something else to worry about."

The woman paused. "Do you love your wife?"

Suddenly, feelings started welling up—like what it would be like to lose Phyllis. There were definitely things worse than losing your job, he realized.

"Yes," he barely managed to croak. There seemed to be something in his throat. Maybe this woman knew what she was talking about.

"Does she know it?"

Jerry flared a bit. "Yes, she does," he insisted with a hint of indignation.

Ms. Tompkins smiled again. "Well, you're probably not alexithymic."

"*Alexi*—what?"

"*Alexithymic*. It means being unable to express feelings—literally, 'no words for emotions.' We sometimes call it flat affect. With people who are out of work, it's usually a temporary condition, but it can be incapacitating until you deal with those feelings and work through them."

Jerry nodded. "So, what's happening to me is normal, as a result of losing my job?"

"Look at it this way," the woman suggested. "Did you lose your job—or did your job lose you?"

For the first time that day, Jerry smiled. Maybe for the first time in days.

The next day was Jerry's first full day at the center. The morning was spent learning his way around the facility, meeting the instructor, and accessing the computer database. The afternoon was spent in a classroom with some instruction and small group breakouts.

Jerry wasn't sure whether the morning or the afternoon was the more enlightening. He found that the computer lab was a place he might spend some time learning some new skills. Today he used the interactive workstation with a touch-screen allowing him to access a wide variety of related subjects. Since Juanita Tompkins had piqued his curiosity about the trick bag of repressed emotions, this was the subject area he chose to pursue. The process reminded him of the bank phone lines or voice-mail systems that prompt callers to select numbered options in a decision tree.

He chose to track subjects related to unemployment, stress, and family problems and was surprised by some of the things he found:

- Jerry was not alone. Each year a million middle-aged American men—aged thirty-five to fifty-four—were losing their jobs at a time when their

personal and family responsibilities are the greatest, giving a whole new meaning to the term
"midlife crisis." Middle-aged men had become the
most inviting targets because of their higher pay.

- Closely related to job loss was a high incidence of
  depression, panic attacks, and drug and alcohol
  abuse. Researchers at the University of Western
  Ontario found that about a third of unemployed
  Canadians interviewed in their study experienced
  serious emotional problems.

- Other studies showed a correlation between
  unemployment and increases in anger, intense
  marital conflict, inconsistent parenting, and even
  child abuse and neglect. And children themselves
  suffered from self-blame, lowered self-esteem,
  confusion, insecurity, worry, withdrawal, depression, anger, and irritability, which often resulted
  in increased misbehavior.

Jerry thought about how it seemed that Phyllis and
their two teenagers, Jason and Judy, had been picking on
him. Adding insult to injury, they even accused *him* of being
mean and ill-tempered. It hadn't made sense. Why was he
being so misunderstood? He knew he'd probably been a little
grouchy at first. Maybe now he was being perceived that
way all the time, rightly or wrongly. It was worth a thought.

In the afternoon their instructor, Howard Somerville,
told Jerry and the dozen other participants that they still had
jobs: "Your job right now is finding another job." Howard
introduced them to the reference works available to job
seekers, explaining that there were more than twelve thousand different job classifications.

Jerry flipped through some of these thick references,
the *Dictionary of Occupational Titles*, the *Guide for Occupational Exploration*, and the *Occupational Outlook Hand-*

book. They were the size of big-city telephone books. If there were that many other fields, he thought, maybe he could find something by changing his career path. Maybe Howard or somebody else at this place could explain how that could be done.

"The way of finding a job these days has changed," Howard told the group. "It used to be that you could find most of the available jobs by checking the classified ads, job postings, and company human resource departments. Not so anymore. Those only account for one-fourth of the available jobs today. So, if you're just applying for the jobs you see in the Sunday paper, you're missing about three-fourths of them. That three-fourths is what we call the 'hidden job market.' That takes some directed strategies to reach, such as networking, that we are going to discuss."

Networking means taking stock of your circle of friends and associates—which is probably a lot larger than you think, he told them. And when you count *their* friends and associates, it can add up to countless potential opportunities. Howard challenged the group to swallow their pride and alert the people in their networks to their plight. Chances are, he said, someone out there knows about a golden employment opportunity—and someone you should talk to about it. Most people are more than happy to help, especially as the downsizing/layoff problem has become commonplace.

The average person has accumulated from five hundred to a thousand personal contacts, he said. That means each connection between two individuals yields between 25,000 (500 times 500) and a million (1,000 times 1,000) potential contacts. He illustrated the power of the network with an experiment by social psychologist Stanley Milgram, who asked randomly selected people in Kansas and Nebraska to try to reach specific unknown individuals in Massachusetts through their networks. While observers guessed it might take a hundred such contacts to reach the intended destination, the average in Milgram's experiment was five and a half—and as few as two.[1]

The moral of the story, Howard said, is that when it comes to finding a job, it's both what you know *and* who you know—or who someone you know knows. For many people, the network has proven to be the single most reliable way of finding the next opportunity. Don't delay listing your contacts and making those phone calls, he said. And don't make the mistake of failing to give feedback to the person who helped you, he added. Let the person know and convey your thanks. It will make that person feel good about continuing to help you.

Then he threw the subject out for discussion. "Why do you suppose the vast majority of job opportunities are hidden?"

A very talkative older man at another table raised his hand. "I don't know what they do with the good jobs, but those aren't the ones they advertise. I can tell you that from personal experience. I think the whole reason they have to advertise them in the first place is they can't find anybody with those qualifications or there's something wrong with the job, like the pay or the working conditions or the company itself."

Howard nodded. "Yeah. Want ads have been good for some specific fields like data processing, but otherwise there's often a reason they have to advertise those jobs. Increasingly, the good jobs are filled by word-of-mouth through personal contacts, often through other employees. If you're an employee, managers know you're only going to recommend somebody who's really good because your credibility is on the line too. Also, word-of-mouth is faster and cheaper. That means as a job-seeker you have to do the same thing yourself that the employers are doing—network. You have to learn the art of self-marketing."

Jerry wasn't terribly surprised. He'd been doing the Sunday classified-ad routine for months, and he'd had a feeling he was missing the boat. But in his bummed-out frame of mind, he kind of didn't care half the time. Maybe that wasn't such a good attitude.

Howard asked them to look at their information sheets. They showed the fastest-growing and fastest-declining occupations, as projected by the U.S. Bureau of Labor Statistics through the year 2005. Several titles jumped out at him. Not too far down the page of fastest-declining occupations, almost as high as "directory assistance operators," was his old trade, "compositors and typesetters, precision." And high on the other list of fastest-growing was "electronic pagination systems workers," the people who had knocked him out of his last job. In fact, it was tenth in the whole country. It figured.

Maybe that's the field I should get into, Jerry thought, although it made him feel somehow a little disloyal to his old trade, which was probably a bit silly. That was like feeling sentimental about yesterday's newspaper instead of turning a new page on today's. In the back of his mind, Jerry also harbored a notion that his occupational salvation might come somehow through computers. It was something, at least, he'd have to check out.

Just then, someone began ringing a bell out in the hall. Jerry wondered at first if it was a fire alarm, but it sounded more like a hand bell, like the old-fashioned brass kind they used to have in the public schools.

"What's that?" said the older man sitting across the table from Jerry. Others were looking around too.

Howard was smiling. "One of our graduates just got a job. Has anyone seen the movie *It's a Wonderful Life,* with Jimmy Stewart?"

A number of hands went up.

"In the movie they'd ring a bell in heaven whenever an angel got his wings. Here, we ring the bell whenever someone gets a job. You'll get used to hearing that around here."

Jerry realized he was smiling again. That made twice in two days.

That afternoon the twelve participants were asked to break up into three subgroups and discuss case studies of several people who had been thrown out of work with slim prospects of getting rehired, largely because of age and out-dated skills. Jerry was most appalled by the insensitive treatment these people had received from their former employers. A fifty-five-year-old woman figuratively received her pink slip in remote fashion along with several other co-workers over the public address system in their work room. A forty-five-year-old man was asked to clean out his desk with a supervisor looking on and then was escorted out the front door by a security officer.

Howard had asked them to come up with some of the feelings these people must have had, and the words poured forth. Betrayal. Fear. Worthlessness. Self-hate. Pity. Withdrawal. Helplessness. Desperation. Anxiety. Shame.

"Anger!" Jerry called out emphatically.

There was an awkward moment of silence as heads turned his way. Jerry swallowed hard. Maybe he'd said it a little loudly. He was surprised to find himself feeling a little warm around the collar. He wasn't just imagining the anger of these other people; he was feeling some of his own ire.

"Well," he added, lowering his voice. "These people were treated like they were less than human, like they had done something wrong—or like criminals, even."

A black woman about his age named Jasmine nodded. "Like dogs."

An older man named George frowned. "I came back from vacation and found my desk had been cleaned out. Nobody knew what had become of my stuff. They just told me I didn't work there anymore."

A younger fellow named Jeff smiled, but his voice sounded almost menacing. "Makes you understand what happens with some of those postal workers."

Jerry found himself bitterly agreeing, but he was somewhat aghast at his own reactions. What was happening to him? Was he going off the deep end? Surely he would never approve of violence. But he could understand what Jeff was getting at. Did that make him a bad guy? Jerry was definitely confused. He wasn't sure how he was supposed to feel, but it wasn't as if he had that much control over it.

When Howard ended the discussion, he suggested that some of them may have been able to relate to the stories they'd discussed. He hoped that some of them might even be able to discuss their own feelings.

"How many of you find it easy to talk to your friends and family about these things?" he asked.

There were no hands.

"Why not?" Howard asked.

"They don't understand," said a man named Cody. "They haven't been through it. They just say, 'Don't worry. Everything will be OK.' Or worse, 'Why don't you just go out and find a job?'"

Howard nodded. "That seems to be what happens. It's called minimizing. With all good intentions, people tend to encourage us to bottle up our feelings when we really need to work them out. Somehow they may think that's being helpful. But how do you feel as a result?"

"Isolated!" someone called out.

"That's right," Howard continued. "But I think some of you found it was easier to open up with strangers here in your small groups because they understand what you're going through."

Jerry remembered how he'd felt when he said the word *anger* and recalled Juanita Tompkins's words the day before. Maybe he *was* angrier than he realized or allowed himself to feel.

Now Howard was writing on the chalkboard. "Rejection. Job loss is all about rejection. Here's one model for understanding your relational style, especially in terms of how you deal with feelings of rejection. Some of it's taken from a book called *Neanderthals at Work*, and some of it is taken from a Christian counseling expert named Neil Anderson.

"You can be a Competitor or a Believer or a Rebel. The Competitor is a controller who handles things by trying to *beat the system*—whether it's school or work or society in general. He is self-sufficient, but he is unable to express his feelings and struggles with perfectionism and worry. The Believer tries to get life *through the system* and so is cut to the heart by rejection, alternating between anger and feelings of worthlessness and poor self-esteem, to say the least."

Jerry froze. He felt as if Howard were reading about him.

"Then there's the Rebel," Howard continued. "As his name says, the Rebel *rebels against the system*. He fights the fire of rejection with fire of his own. 'You can't fire me—I quit!' he would say, even if he cuts off his own nose and burns his own bridges, ending up without severance or unemployment benefits. The Rebel struggles with a great deal of bitterness toward others as well as self-hatred."

A younger Hispanic woman named Maria raised her hand with a question. "Can you be more than one type? I identify with all three of those."

"Absolutely," said Howard, smiling. "Most of us are predominantly one type, but we may move in and out of the others, depending on our circumstances and what seems to meet our needs at the moment."

Jerry leaned back heavily. There was a lot to think about, an awful lot. But at least there was some assurance in knowing that others had been there before and there were ways of dealing with these sorts of things. Maybe he didn't have to be a victim of his own reactions, with the world pushing his preprogrammed buttons. It even helped knowing that there were others worse off than himself. *At least,* he thought, *I know I'm not alone.*

NOTE

1. Stanley Milgram et al., *The Individual in a Social World: Essays and Experiments* (New York: McGraw-Hill, 1992), 259–75.

8

SURVIVAL AND SELF-MARKETING

Over the next three days our mythical Jerry Davenport received a wealth of practical information about searching for a new job. For the first two days he learned about survival skills and goal setting and how to write a personal mission statement, a résumé, a Minute Pitch, and an action plan. On the third day he came to grips with a new direction for his life by reinventing his career.

The following is an account of those three days.

SURVIVAL SKILLS

Think of a career like a car, Howard told Jerry's group. Being out of a job is like driving on a curve. If you don't slow down, there's going to be trouble. Same thing with your lifestyle. If you try to keep up the same standard of living after losing your job, you're going to put too much pressure on yourself and possibly wipe out financially. Unemployment compensation is not great income. It's not supposed to be. It's only supposed to be a temporary safety net for survival. And bankruptcy is no fun. You need to reduce your expenditures quickly.

The higher the lost income, the longer it may take to replace. One rule of thumb is an average of one month for every $10,000 of lost pay. So you could expect to take about three months to find a comparable job if you're a typical blue-collar worker, maybe around six months for higher-paid professionals, and even a year or more for high-level business executives. Knowing that, you shouldn't get frustrated and discouraged if you don't land a job the first couple of weeks. But neither should you become complacent, especially if you see excessive time passing by.

In addition to rejection/dejection, you and your family may suffer from a sense of *deprivation*. It may seem unfair, but you are going to have less wherewithal in your time of greatest need. It's all a matter of perspective. In pioneer days, people worked long enough to meet their basic needs for food, clothing, and shelter, and then they did other things, like rest or recreate. Subsistence meant working until you had enough, then stopping. But since the Industrial Revolution and the factory-model workplace, our work lives have become prepackaged increments of time and pay, creating mass-produced expectations of houses, cars, wardrobes, gadgets, and other consumables. Then there's Madison Avenue's "market-induced demand," which gets us desiring things we don't even need. Then when we have to give things up, we feel deprived in comparison to what we've grown used to and what the rest of our world considers the norm.

But is the norm "normal"? "Enough" has become something entirely different from what it once was. We are now locked into an artificial standard of living of high expectations—the American ideal of affluence, creature comfort, and instant gratification—that leaves frustration in its absence. We may not be able to turn the clock back to an earlier century, but we can reduce our cost of living and down-scale, conserve, and economize—i.e., slow down before we wipe out on the curve.

Freedom is *not* being trapped by a personal debt load of more than $10,000 in consumer debt (beyond home mort-gage), as is the typical U.S. family. When most of that is on credit cards, it can become an enslavement because we may become unable to pay any more than the minimum monthly charge and no longer be able to reduce the principal. Even with a regular income, that's a problem. When that person becomes unemployed, it can be financially disastrous. Howard gave the group some handouts consisting of a fami-ly budget work sheet, a list of household expenses that could be cut or reduced, and samples of suggested letters that can be sent to creditors proposing a deferred payment schedule.

Use common sense, Howard told the group. You're not the first people to be laid off. Businesspeople are well aware of the downsizing/layoff phenomenon. In the busi-ness world, vendors are used to waiting ninety days for pay-ment from customers. Many times creditors can be persuaded to accept deferred payment, especially if they sense you are sincere. And this is certainly more honorable than default-ing on the debt entirely.

Meanwhile, you can control the damage from this point on and stop the bleeding by reducing expenses. Put away your credit cards. Cut them up and throw them away if they control you instead of vice versa. It may be easier said than done, but you can eliminate everything but the necessities—heat, food, shelter, health care, and so on. Necessities do *not* include cable TV, carry-out pizza, maga-zine subscriptions, compact disks, athletic club member-ships, and new clothes. But it *might* include a new business outfit if that's what it takes to get a new job.

This is the time to get serious. You may question having cable service shut off if you think you might get a job in a few weeks, but these days the average wait is much longer than that. By the time you're proved wrong, it's too late. You may be able to return a sweater you shouldn't have bought, but you can't *un*watch three months of cable TV or *un*eat a bunch of carryout meals. It may also seem like such small economies that you question what difference they could make. But taken together as a whole, they can be quite significant. You are going to have a hard enough time paying the old bills accumulated prior to your discharge, let alone incurring new expenses.

Miscellaneous:

☑ Don't burn your bridges. Resist the impulse to bad-mouth your former employer to his face or behind his back. You may be able to obtain a helpful letter of reference if your discharge was not your fault and you left on amicable terms. This can give you tremendous credibility with any prospective employer who might otherwise be concerned about hiring a potential problem person. Employers will understand that you were just an ordinary casualty, like thousands of others.

☑ Treat looking for work like a job. Think of it as an assignment and avoid the "hundred-pound telephone" and "twenty-pound tongue" problem that plagues job-seekers. Don't succumb to the "night owl" temptation. Get out of bed in the morning and keep regular business hours. While few people can stomach working the telephone or pounding the pavement for eight-hour stretches, a significant portion of the work week should be devoted to the work search. You might want to reserve one day of the week for a different project—like finally painting the house, doing your genealogy, or attending your child's choir concert—and using the other four for job-hunting.

Part-time volunteerism, especially if it puts you in contact with those less fortunate than yourself, can be a wonderful tonic. Mondays, which are often the most discouraging day for jobless people, are great for this sort of thing.

☑ Identify your top professional and personal goals and write them down on a time line—i.e., three months, six months, a year. Your primary goal is to find employment, but that should not be your only goal. Otherwise, your daily mind-set until you reach that goal may be failure. Have some reasonable secondary goals that are doable to cultivate a success mind-set. Losing forty or fifty pounds might be admirable, but the likelihood of failure may only raise your stress level or compound your woes. Just establishing an exercise regimen, no matter how modest, may be more realistic. Goal areas to consider include family, friends, associates, income, savings, investments, purchases, fitness, health, appearance, nutrition, recreation, relaxation, training, education, travel, and hobbies. Spend some time nurturing your relationship with your spouse, which might be under considerable stress. If you do these things right, the period of unemployment need not be "lost" time.

Some of these principles are foundational. Once you have identified both short- and long-range goals, you can begin constructing a specific action plan employing your personal values, skills, and interests. For example, if you identify a new vocational field to pursue, you might find you need to acquire some additional skills, which means your action plan should include a strategy for obtaining some further education or training.

Your Personal Mission

Why should you write a personal mission statement? Because its content can be key to the other statements you will need to make in your employment search—from an action plan to a résumé to a short personal presentation. Even if no one else were ever to see this statement, just going through the thought process is worthwhile. Apart from simple honesty, there are no wrong answers. Think in terms of "the purpose for which I was put here on earth." Then you can get more specific in vocational terms.

Jerry turned in his first stab at a personal mission statement, and the next day Juanita helped him to phrase it better. Jerry Davenport's Mission Statement:

I am devoted to the publishing of mass-circulation periodicals through the physical creation of the printed page. I enjoy producing high-quality publications with graphics and text that bring helpful information, entertainment, and amusement to thousands of people. I work best as a team player in a large organization in a creative, nonsupervisory capacity. I am committed first and foremost to the welfare of my family and am willing to change jobs or careers as necessary, but prefer not to have night shifts or travel that would take me from my family.

Juanita said, yes, mission or purpose statements can and should change over time in detail as circumstances and your understanding change, but the primary thrust should endure. That's why she steered Jerry away from stating a specific field such as stereotyper or keyliner. She looked at the doodlings in his notebook and asked if he had ever done anything in the art field. He told her he used to draw a lot for fun but had never pursued it seriously. Juanita suggested that he take some tests that might indicate whether something like graphic design might be a career option for him, since he was interested in the three main ingredients—publishing, computers, and design.

In class, Howard asked the group to take their mission statements and apply them to the creation of a résumé. Jerry had a résumé of sorts that was just a list of previous jobs. It definitely needed upgrading. The class learned how to craft an initial "Objective" statement at the top that is half job wanted, half mission statement of no more than two dozen words. An example of an Objective statement from an abstracter/indexer for business and technical publications: "A support position in a library or publishing center using my proven research, organizational, and training skills to contribute to effective information transfer."

This statement's strength is that it isn't "gimme, gimme"-oriented. It will appeal to employers because it emphasizes not so much what the applicant wants to get out of the company as what he or she would *contribute* to the work or the organization. In that light, the Jerry Davenport résumé Objective should state: "*A position in the publishing field where I can be an effective team member in the production of high-quality publications with text and graphics.*" That is specific enough to get the point across, but general enough to keep his options open for a different division within the same occupational field—such as graphic design or electronic pagination systems, assuming he were to get the additional training.

As for the rest of the résumé, Jerry's old version was like the "chronological" résumé with his work history listed in reverse order from most recent to earliest. Besides an initial Objective, Howard suggested that Jerry add a Summary of Qualifications and a Related Experiences section. Qualifications—the first place many employers look—should describe several abilities and skills, such as the equipment he knows how to operate and the tasks he is trained to perform, such as page pasteup and layout. The specific training or education itself would be listed elsewhere under its own separate section. Related Experiences could be optional or miscellaneous items, such as other accomplishments, awards, affiliations, organizations, workshops, associations, and relevant volunteer work.

A different version of the résumé is the "functional" format, which is organized according to skill or experience categories rather than time periods, Howard told the group. It can be useful when you have made career changes or there are gaps in your work history. The downside is that employers may think you are hiding something, such as a jail term. Yet another version, the "combination" format, takes the best of the chronological and functional formats. It is done either by adding an Experience section to the functional format to feature the work history or by emphasizing accomplishments within each unit of the chronological list. The combination format has become popular because of its versatility.

Whatever the format, your résumé needs to grab the potential employer's attention and be effortless to read. It is a self-marketing tool, potentially the most powerful one you have, and is a warm-up for the employment interview. Whereas an employment application tells the employer what he wants to know, the résumé lets the applicant turn the tables to choose the information he wants to present. Some companies now are storing scanned images of employment applications and résumés in their computer systems, referenced by key words or phrases related to the company's objectives. How to capitalize on that: If the company is advertising a position, check the ad for specific wording of the qualifications sought and adjust your résumé accordingly. With the right words, you might just show up on the right VDT screen at the right time.

Experts disagree on résumé length, Howard said. Some say employers don't want to see anything longer than one page, whereas others say not to try to cram everything onto one page. Probably safe advice is to condense where practical, especially where it helps readability. If it's not that much over a page, condense some more until it fits onto one page. Professional résumé services can help for a fee, but the results will only be as good as the information and direction you provide the service. They shouldn't be expected to get the right emphasis where you have been less than clear.

If you don't get professional help, at least have another pair of good eyes look at the résumé before it goes anywhere. Misspellings, bad grammar, typographical errors, sloppiness, and other errors will be held against you—fairly or not—as a reflection of your work ethic. On the other hand, a good résumé may not directly land you a job, but it can help you survive at least the first cut as the employer reduces his mountain of applications.

After fixing up their résumés, the group constructed their Minute Pitches. These are for situations where you have only a very short time to make your case to someone in the process of networking and making phone contacts and even in an actual job interview, Howard said. It is your core message and is sometimes called by other names, including the "Short Personal Presentation," the "Thirty-Second Commercial," and the "Ninety-Second Self-Presentation." Since it is a form of direct marketing appeal, it should adhere to the time-honored salesman's success formula, AIDA—attempting to arouse the listener's Attention, Interest, Desire, and Action. That means it should be more than just informational content for the intellect, but should appeal to the will and even emotions. The visceral level is where acceptance/rejection decisions about people are often made.

The savvy job prospector will apply the distinction between features and benefits to his own product—himself. The *features* of a microwave oven, for example, might include a rotating carousel or multidirectional heating element. The *benefit*, however, is more even heat distribution to prevent hot and cold spots. Obviously, the benefit will be more attractive to the prospective customer than just the feature. And that essentially is what you're asking the prospective employer to do—i.e., make a purchasing decision. Other features being equal in terms of training and skills, what benefit might you represent over another applicant? Often, these benefits are intangible things, such as attitude and values. Employers frequently rank attitude as a tiebreaker in their hiring decisions. If you have a bad attitude, fix it. If you have a good one, promote it.

The three basic elements of the Minute Pitch are name, abilities (values, skills, interests), and accomplishments. That's pretty simple, but it's a pretty short statement. Employers want to hear action-oriented statements. Think of what benefits or contributions you may have made in your previous jobs, such as meeting deadlines, saving money, making a profit, having an idea, or creating a new product or service. How was the company better off for your involvement? A few suggested action words include maximized, designed, coordinated, initiated, implemented, maintained, operated, improved, expedited, constructed, eliminated, controlled, created, developed, directed, fixed, implemented, increased, completed, changed, achieved, administered, and assembled.

This short personal presentation should be rehearsed with a partner until it sounds natural, credible, sincere, clear, and persuasive, Howard said. That done, you're almost ready for the main event—the actual job interview. This process arms you with the answer to one of the "killer questions" in job interviews: "Tell me about yourself." It's called a "killer" question because its maddening simplicity has caused otherwise sensible people either to go blank and speechless or to babble ad nauseam. But having thought through the process of a personal mission statement, an objective statement, and a Minute Pitch, there's no good reason for your tongue to embarrass you.

Two other killer questions, according to an article in the *National Business Employment Weekly* by Ken Glickman, an executive with Right Associates, a national business outplacement firm, are "Why did you leave your last job?" and "What do you really want to do?"[1] The only one you should fear is why you left your last job. The interviewer's ulterior motive may be just to see how you handle a question that makes most people squirm a bit. Again, resist any temptation to bad-mouth your previous employer. This is a name-rank-and-serial-number question—i.e., you are only obligated to explain if you quit the job. If your employer terminated it, you can give an official reason—downsizing, etc.—and beyond that only the employer can explain the employer's actions.

When it comes to what you really want to do, you now should have this nailed down better than anyone else this interviewer has interviewed. Go for it.

POSTSCRIPT

I haven't heard from Jerry recently, but Juanita Tompkins said it's a good prognosis. After some additional testing, she urged Jerry to consider going into graphic design. He agreed, and, with the help of federal funding from the Job Training Partnership Act, he has enrolled in classes at the local community college toward that end.

It looks like Jerry Davenport's couch potato days may be coming to an end.

NOTE

1. Ken Glickman, "Learn to Handle 'Killer' Interview Questions," *National Business Employment Weekly*, 4 February 1996.

9

ALTERNATIVES

very morning Ralph A. Dise, Jr., wakes up unemployed. He's been doing that every day since 1985—June 22, 1985, to be exact. That's the day he lost his corporate job at the reorganizing LTV Steel Company in Cleveland. But in Dise's case, being unemployed means anything but being out of work. He has his own business as a professional outplacement consultant.

"The difference between you and me," he told a roomful of managerial and executive job prospectors at Cleveland's Career Initiatives Center, "is that when you come here every day, you are looking for one customer. I have to look for many customers. No single customer can sustain my business. I need maybe forty or fifty customers a year. If you are unemployed, you are actually self-employed."

That one customer is the traditional employer. Dise encourages job prospectors to cultivate a self-employed attitude even after finding a new job. Self-employment may not be for everybody, but everybody needs to have a self-employed attitude. More than that, for a growing number of people, the answer may be more than adopting a self-employed attitude, but actually becoming self-employed.

For me, the lightbulb went on after my second career went down in flames. The first one—journalism—lasted twenty years, long enough for three different jobs. But by 1987, when I began looking for my fourth newspaper position, something had changed. In the 1970s, I used to get nice, personalized, hand-signed letters from editors telling me there were no openings, but they'd keep my application on file. This time, there were no such letters. In fact, I was disturbed to find that it was the rare exception to get the courtesy of *any* response, even when I was applying for actual openings advertised in the *Editor & Publisher* trade journal. I tended to assume that this was a recent development peculiar to my profession.

My second career—public relations—lasted only six years. One Monday morning I came in at nine and was literally out on the street by nine-thirty. The guy after me was out by ten. Since then, I have been told there's a neologism for that, too—being "streeted." I immediately began looking for a replacement job and began to experience, as Yogi Berra is alleged to have said, "déjà vu all over again." PR had become another bear market. The few available positions I could find to apply for in my town paid so little that I began to consider something that had been only an attractive pipe dream before—working for myself, being my own boss.

I soon found that there might not be many good jobs, but there was a good deal of work available if I knew where to look for it. The CEO of a local public relations/advertising agency, for example, acquired several new clients, but said he was leery of staffing up aggressively for the long term. Giving me some assignments as an independent contractor helped both him and me. Then, to my surprise, my former employer offered me the same arrangement on a larger scale, and this company ironically became the biggest client of Adams Business Communications. ABC, in turn, provided me the base from which to strike out in some other directions.

I did some freelance writing for business publications, which has been better for my professional development, visibility, and education than for pure income. (Tip: Self-employment is more lucrative if you charge on the billable-hour rather than flat-fee basis, as writers are more usually paid. Unless you can do an exceptionally fast turnaround, flat fees get eaten up quickly in time-intensive projects like writing and communications.) I also continued to write books, which was personally rewarding but compounded the problem experienced by self-employed people everywhere, especially in start-up situations: *long* hours. But if the investment stage proves successful in the long run, it will have been worth it.

ABC also served as the launchpad for a second enterprise that could end up eclipsing the first—a management consulting service called WorkLife, Inc. This service is aimed at helping managers and employees find fulfillment in the work itself through an improved work environment and corporate culture. My partner, a former labor negotiator named Sam Lombardo, lost his job five months after I lost mine. When we first started discussing the WorkLife concept, which involves a unique, if not radical, methodology, Sam and I were both employed and would never have had the courage—or recklessness—to quit our jobs to start such a venture. He was newly married with a baby on the way, and I was months away from sending my oldest child to college. The timing was what's sometimes called counterintuitive. Translation: A sane person would not have planned it that way.

But unemployment gave us the boost that we needed. The job is dead—long live the new career!

NEWTON'S COROLLARY

It was a different world when C. Northcote Parkinson published his delightful little book, *Parkinson's Law*, in 1958. U.S. and British businesses were fat and happy, and lifetime employment was the norm. Parkinson's first law states: "Work expands to fill the time available for its completion." The book was a good-natured poke at the bureaucratic inefficiencies of that old paradigm, with all of its meetings, committees, recreation leagues, speakers' bureaus, and gold watches, before there was any reason for entire industries to fear for their corporate survival or to worry about a foreign competitor walking away with the marbles.

As we now know all too well, it was that complacent attitude that inadvertently paved the way for those predatory incursions in the first place. Today, that hidebound view would be like wading into an Amazon River tributary and waiting for the piranha to gather. The new reality might be more like a paraphrase of one of the laws of thermodynamics: *"Jobs may come and go, but work is neither created nor destroyed. It is only changed in form."* I am calling it "Newton's Corollary" in honor of the great English mathematician.

What are these new opportunities, this work in new forms? There are actually quite a few: temporary employment, outsourcing, job sharing, composite careers, hoteling, telecommuting, home-based business, self-employment, independent contracting, adhocracies, strategic partnerships, electronic commerce, the virtual corporation, the virtual office, even virtual products. Newton's Corollary is confirmed by the fact that, despite all of the attention given to the downsizing/layoff phenomenon, the unemployment rate has been stable. Considerably less publicity has attended the appearance of new jobs. "Fired workers can be rehired more quickly in a growing economy," wrote *Newsweek* columnist Robert J. Samuelson (March 25, 1996).[1]

The largest nongovernmental employer in the United

States today is Manpower, Inc., the agency for temporary workers. Temps or contingency workers in general now account for 29 percent of the U.S. workforce or 35 million people, according to the U.S. Bureau of Labor Statistics. And these are no longer confined to secretarial, clerical, and other support personnel, but comprise an increasingly diverse workforce, including engineers, legal and medical workers, and other professional services. Some beauty salons are even paying temporary workers to give permanents.

Former corporate executioner Alan Downs says it's time for a new social contract recognizing current realities in the marketplace, including an emerging class of workers he calls PICs—professional independent contract employees—or contract professionals. PICs resemble temps, but Downs argues they should command higher fees even than permanent employees because they bear the responsibility for their own benefits (health, life, and retirement), professional development, self-marketing, and downtime between projects.

Downs writes in *Corporate Executions:*

> Changing the corporation from a roster of employees to a loosely connected network of contract professionals will dramatically shrink the size in number of employees and space of today's corporation. With this shrinking will come a shift in responsibility from the shoulders of the corporation to the workers. No longer will the company bear the time-consuming, parental responsibility for providing the material needs of its workers; nor will it be required to police their day-to-day activities. Instead, the company can focus time and attention on essential business strategy.[2]

Indeed, the concept is not all that new. Building contractors, craftsmen, carpenters, and painters, as Downs points out, have been working like this for years. And now consultants and independent contractors like me are doing it as well. What's new is the challenge to our society, not just to accept it as a growing way of life, but to make provision for such work within the mainstream of our economy. To Alan Downs's proposal, I give a hearty amen. I had to give up collecting *any* state unemployment benefits after a few weeks of trying unsuccessfully to adjust that against the sporadic and unpredictable income I was starting to generate as a freelancer. Losing that safety net certainly accelerated my move to become self-sufficient! In so many ways—from taxes to benefits to government red tape on things like home offices—the life of an independent contractor does not entirely compute yet in America.

HOME, INC.

The fact that headcount-conscious, downsizing U.S. corporations are turning increasingly to outsourcing fulfills the prediction of Newton's Corollary by creating enormous new opportunities for entrepreneurs and the growing class of professional independent contractors that Alan Downs describes. In many ways, the historic trend in the relationship between work and life is coming full circle, to the point of giving entirely new meaning to the term "cottage industry."

Companies large and small are being affected by these changes in corporate culture and personal lifestyle. The Big Six accounting firm of Ernst & Young, for example, has adopted *hoteling* for some workers. Instead of being assigned offices and working behind desks, the company's management consultants in some cities spend most of their time out at client sites. When they are in the office, they are assigned working space in some common office areas set aside for the purpose. Elsewhere, infotech equipment, such as laptop computers and cellular modems, make it increasingly possible to perform many jobs from anywhere, including a home or a car.

Somewhere between 6 and 10 million Americans are *telecommuters*—i.e., they are still employed but work off-site through telecommunications, usually at home. Telecommuters are the fastest-growing segment of the work-at-home force, according to Link Resources Corp., a research firm that provides statistics for the National Association of Home Based Businesses. Some experts expect this number to double by the year 2000. Others estimate that by the new century one-fourth of Americans will work from home full-time, including both telecommuters and self-employed people. Already nearly a third of the workforce (39 million people) do some portion of their work at home.

Interestingly, efficiency-minded American business is discovering that in many cases the person who works at home is actually more productive than the one in the office. An average 15 to 20 percent increase in productivity has been associated with working at home. Factors include fewer interruptions and distractions than in the traditional workplace with all of its meetings, announcements, paperwork, and watercooler chitchat. But it would be premature to pronounce the traditional work environment obsolete. Clearly, working at home is only applicable to certain types of enterprise, generally in the area of services—such as computer and other information workers, accountants, sales reps, insurance adjusters, and market research analysts. It's probably a safe bet that it will be a long time before any Fords will be built in the typical basement.

There is also the intangible human factor. Those who have been working at home to date may be those most equipped and motivated to do so, and therefore more likely to succeed. As their ranks grow approximately 20 percent a year, only time will tell if this trend holds up. Telecommuters, for example, have to justify themselves to their bosses and co-workers with hard results to avoid the unspoken suspicion of lounging about. The self-employed at home have a more direct incentive: Produce or don't eat.

There is no organizational safety net beneath them if they slack off. But, as one who routinely pays those dues, I see nothing wrong with being responsible for myself. Anything else is probably doomed to fail in the long run, anyway.

I will be the first to admit that the home office environment or self-employment is not for everybody. To paraphrase the old saying about the lawyer who represents himself: "The worker who goes into business for himself has a fool for a boss." That is to say, quitting your job to work for yourself is no automatic solution to the troubled career. If some of your woes are of your own making or due to your own shortcomings, hiring yourself to be your new boss may do no more than trade one set of problems for another.

Not everyone is sufficiently self-disciplined or self-directed by nature to work alone, just as some people are not by nature team players. According to management consultant and professor Harry Levinson, there are some psychological needs that the workplace provides that are absent at home—principally a sense of achievement and connectedness, the "need to depend on others and be depended upon."[3] Levinson is chairman of the Levinson Institute, Waltham, Massachusetts, which focuses on the psychological aspects of leadership in organizations. These factors are remarkably reminiscent of the first two of our three universal human needs—relationship, impact, and integrity.

Brad Schepp, author of *The Telecommuter's Handbook*, says a sense of isolation and disconnectedness is the biggest drawback for the worker at home. "People who telecommute full-time are especially prone to feeling they are no longer part of the team. Psychologists call this company-connectedness feeling *organizational identification*, and it is important because how much you identify with your company affects how high you'll climb the corporate ladder."[4] Some of that isolation can be combated with commonsense approaches—staying in touch with others by phone, lunch dates, e-mail, and just getting out of the office periodically.

Then there are others who work fine solo but face the opposite problem—too many intrusions and distractions from friends, associates, and other family members. Or maybe it's the temptation to distract themselves by playing computer solitaire, listening to the radio, watching television, surfing the Net, or chatting excessively on the phone. Possessing a vivid imagination for failure, an acute drivenness, and the gift of worrying, I have rarely experienced those distractions for long before I start barking, either at others to back off or at myself to get serious. If anything, my own temptation is the opposite—to let my work life intrude into my personal and family life through crash projects and long hours, which is another classic pitfall.

DEVELOP DISCIPLINE

If you lack natural discipline, I recommend importing some. Doors are wonderful devices for screening things out. If people can't take a hint, post a biohazard sign or some other toxic symbol on the outside. If *you're* the dense one, try posting a picture of your former boss on the inside (at least for a while). That's always good for a reality check. If you don't have a picture of your former boss, hang up a picture of Saddam Hussein or Godzilla and pretend. This is also where goals come in. Set deadlines for yourself, just as you would have if you worked downtown, and withhold incentives—food or work breaks—until you have reached them. But once you have met your goals and deadlines, take time to reward yourself. Now you deserve it.

If you are too driven and your family and friends have forgotten your name, schedule some downtime. If you're too busy to do that, you're too busy. Go back to square one and revisit your personal mission—why you were put here on earth. It probably wasn't to spend more time in the office.

Yes, there are downsides to the post-job lifestyle—or "dejobbing," as William Bridges calls it—but the advantages are just as real. Ri Regina, the former NCR manager, said that even though she's an extrovert, the home office lifestyle suits her as long as she can manage to get outside several times a week.

"I love coming down here and sitting in my office," she said, "and I have got my dog sitting at my feet, I have my bayberry candle burning on my desk, I have my CD player with my collection of CDs from home and the library. I have wonderful music playing all day, the windows open, looking at the soft snow falling. This is great, and I am here in my sweat suit."

Roy Peterson, the former health insurance manager, is particularly fond of not having to wear a tie and fight rush hour traffic.

"There are a number of upsides," he said. "There is a lot less wear and tear on you and your car and your clothes and everything else because you don't have to go anywhere. There are two hours a day you save because you are not in a car just trying to get to the place that you are going to work. That's a lot of time—ten hours a week. So, basically one advantage is you get a day a week back. You don't have to wear a tie.

"There is a lot more flexibility. If my daughter has a track meet at four o'clock, I can probably work things out so I can be there, and no one is going to howl about it and I'll still get as much or more done as I would have otherwise. With the electronic means available to us, you just don't have to go as many places as you used to. It is more comfortable, and it feels good. I get up in the morning and go to work by going down a flight of stairs."

THE VIRTUAL CAREER

It is helpful to think of these different work environments as a continuum. At one end is the traditional workplace with an executive suite, security guards, watercoolers, high-end machinery or office equipment, and suits and ties or hard hats and ear protection. At the other extreme is the sunporch office where a pensive writer in jeans and an absurd orange-and-white cat named Roscoe share an eight-foot-square space with a desk, personal computer, printer, phone, stacks of books, a bottle of antacid tablets, several cacti, and a sprawling spider plant.

In between are the various shades of gray, such as the *telecommuters* and *hotelers,* who are still employed by an organization but work mostly outside. Then there's *job-sharing,* where two part-timers might divide the responsibilities of a full-time position, though probably without the benefits. Some people only want to work for an employer part-time because they are engaged in what's called a *composite career.* These are the people who work different jobs or combine employment with some entrepreneurial enterprise, like the art dealer who works in a machine shop by day.

This is the place on the continuum where self-employment begins, as Ralph Dise says, with multiple bosses called clients and customers. William Bridges urges post-job workers to organize "You & Co." and run it as a business.[5] Almost paradoxically, it combines specialization (defining a narrow market niche for yourself) and diversification (with multiple activities, customers, and income streams). I don't have to look far for an example. My own Adams Business Communications is a diverse umbrella for several activities, including public relations as a subcontractor, freelance business writing, and authoring books and novels.

Increasingly, the line is blurring between traditional businesses and one-man bands like ABC and Net Presence. With state-of-the-art information technology, these *virtual offices* in dens and sunporches are capable of providing services that once would have required leased space and maybe several support personnel. When two or more of these mini-organizations join forces for the purpose of a particular project, it is sometimes called an *adhocracy,* a *strategic alliance,* or a *virtual corporation.* Bob Kasarda's Gemini Productions works this way routinely with another company called Buckel Productions and several independent contractors, including me once. And there have been discussions of similar joint ventures between Visioneering and the WorkLife management consulting service.

That's the shape of things to come. Even stranger is the emergence of *virtual products*—custom-produced goods that do not even exist until customers order them. And increasingly, customers will be ordering them not from a store or snail-mail order, but through the vehicle of *electronic commerce* through a service such as Ri Regina's Buy It On-Line. Earlier this century, the Model-T was available in any color, Henry Ford said, as long at it was black. At the end of the century, Harry Dent says, *customization*—tailoring individual products and services to personal specifications—is the star to follow.

"A new economy is emerging," he wrote in *JobShock.* "I call it the customized economy. This is the biggest trend emerging out of information technologies. It is an economic leap even greater than the assembly line of the past century that allowed an unprecedented array of standardized products to move into mass affordability and a ninefold increase in the average wage adjusted for inflation. What we are going to see in the coming decades is that customized products and services are going to move increasingly into mass affordability. . . . This will be the prime source of job growth and security and profits in business."[6]

☞ **According to Dent, here are some more traditional job categories that lend themselves to home-based business and independent contractors:**

Accounting and bookkeeping; advertising and pro-

motion; art and promotion materials; career counseling and outplacement; editorials and writing; field sales; janitorial and maintenance; market research and analysis; MIS and computer software and systems; personality testing and evaluations; phone sales and telemarketing; secretarial and office production services; tax and tax planning; training and educational materials.[7]

NOTES

1. Robert J. Samuelson, "Down-Sizing for Growth," *Newsweek*, 25 March 1996, 45.
2. Alan Downs, *Corporate Executions* (New York: Amacom, 1995), 206–7.
3. Harry Levinson, quoted in Todd Shryock, "Telecommuting Has Value, but Don't Jump in Too Quickly," *Small Business News Cleveland*, February 1996, 68–69.
4. Brad Schepp, *The Telecommuter's Handbook: How to Work for a Salary—Without Ever Leaving the House* (New York: Pharos, 1990), 23.
5. William Bridges, *JobShift: How to Prosper in a World Without Jobs* (Reading, Mass.: Addison-Wesley, 1994), 109–12.
6. Harry S. Dent, Jr., *JobShock: Four New Principles Transforming Our Work and Business* (New York: St. Martin's, 1995), 53–55.
7. Ibid., 283.

10

THE ULTIMATE MISSION

The average time between job situations, according to some surveys, is nine months—long enough to create new life. Make it a time to find a new life. Employment experts say there are at least two essentials for making a good case to the future employer, and they also may apply to self-employment. Unfortunately, they are two things that the beaten-down victim of the downsizing wave is least likely to possess in abundance—ability to demonstrate competence and an enthusiastic demeanor.

Enthusiasm is a magical word. It comes from the Greek and literally means "to be filled with God" *(theos/theus)*. It may seem a cruel irony that when an individual is most beaten down, he or she must somehow appear the most upbeat and confident to hope to win the favor of another employer. Or, like Ralph Dise, to appeal to multiple employers, called clients and customers. Truly, this would seem to require the intervention of the divine and miraculous.

Some experts suggest getting motivated with clearer values and even spiritual insights by writing your own obituary. List your key accomplishments, what people will remember you for, and the additional things you might yet achieve. "People are always amazed at how few good years they have left," writes David Noer in *Healing the Wounds*.[1] The point is not to become further discouraged, but to appreciate the value of the remaining time and to make the most of it.

This brings us back full circle to our personal mission in life. How do we know when we have found it? Richard Nelson Bolles, author of the famous *What Color Is Your Parachute?* book that is updated annually, is also an Episcopal priest. In the appendix of his books, he states categorically that this search inevitably leads to God—the Caller behind the calling, the Destination at the end of the destiny. The word *mission* itself—from the Latin *mittere*, meaning "to send," as in transmit or remit—implies a Sender. Similarly, *vocation* derives from the Latin "to call," as in "evoke" (to call out) or "revoke" (to call back).

"If you would figure out your Mission in life, you must also be willing to think about God in connection with your job-hunt," Bolles wrote. In fact, Bolles believes each person has *three* missions: discovering God, making this world a better place, and exercising "your greatest gift, which you most delight to use," in your God-given mission.[2] He says that is the talent that "gives us the greatest pleasure from its exercise *(it is usually the one which, when we use it, causes us to lose all sense of time)*."[3]

When I was newly unemployed, I benefited from small daily doses of work/life wisdom from motivational speaker Jim Rohn via a friend's loaner videotape. Rohn's words rang a bell when he likened our role to the planting of an acorn and God's role to growing the oak tree. He reminded his audience of Christ's words about God's care and concern for the birds of the air and the lilies of the field while men "of little faith" worry about what they will eat, drink, and wear. Rohn said this is God's promise that He will grow the tree if we will plant the seed—i.e., exercise our gifts.

Then it hit me as forcefully as if God had spoken to me personally, though inaudibly: "If you want to know God's will for your life, look at your gifts. He doesn't play games; like the acorn, you already have the ability to perform whatever is in God's plan for you." I began to have a greater assurance that I had something better under me than an earthly safety net—what Scripture calls the "everlasting arms."

Human resources consultant Ralph T. Mattson wrote in *Redeemed Ambition:* "Very important signposts in the matter of selecting careers are the gifts He has willed into your personalities. God's definition of a person is the act of creating him. . . . All the information with which we need to begin the process of career selection already resides within us. We must tap it."[4]

The problem is not that we don't believe in God. Gallup polls indicate that 94 percent of Americans have such a belief; 90 percent even pray. The problem is in our "little faith." In some ways, Bolles and others suggest, the problem may even be worse for believers. We ask, "How could God let this happen to me, if He truly loved me?" I know I felt that way after the death of my son. It's called a sense of abandonment.

In a sometimes disturbing and always challenging book, *Bold Love,* Dan Allender argues that our attitude toward God at these times is most akin to actual hatred. We take for granted our unfettered right to exercise free will, but then tacitly accuse God of abandoning us by not intervening when misfortune befalls us. If bitterness and grudges on the human plane sap our strength and rot our bones, what about the spiritual dimension? Neil Anderson says flatly that in his counseling unforgiveness is the number one avenue for occult oppression—in *believers.* Allender says when faced with injustice and suffering in the world we have a basic choice in our response between hatred versus gratitude. We can respond to life's circumstances with "humble, quiet grace" or "angry, demanding assertion."[5]

God the great Sustainer does not cause our hard times, nor does He generally rescue us out of them. But He does give us the grace, courage, and strength to endure hard times. Many times, that's the factory that produces those character qualities. "The 94% of us who believe in God," Bolles wrote, "usually need a larger conception of God, as we face each new crisis in our life. If you've got an old faith hanging in the closet of your mind, now would be a good time to take it out and dust it off."[6]

Easy for him to say? Not really. Richard Bolles is the brother of Don Bolles, an investigative reporter in Arizona who was killed by a car bomb in 1976 while investigating organized crime and political connections. As a newspaper reporter then myself, I remember Don Bolles's agonizing eleven-day demise. It was the inspiration for the founding of an organization called IRE—Investigative Reporters and Editors—which I joined. May I suggest that Richard Bolles is intimately acquainted with injustice and suffering. He too has faced the choice between humble, quiet grace and angry, demanding assertion and has chosen wisely. That wise choice has resulted in an enormous overflow into the lives of others such as myself.

What is the application? Forgive: Forgive the one who fired you. It may be a blessing in disguise in the form of a new future. Forgive yourself. Now is the time you need to stand your tallest—acquiring a nobler character full of grace, courage, and strength. Get right with God. Think of the things for which you have been forgiven. He is the light-house. Change *your* heading.

No Earthly Security

Life is full of surprises. Like going to work one day

and being told your services are no longer required. Most of us prefer a little more predictability in our affairs. We even come to demand that events follow a prescribed course, and when things stray from the script, we become angry and frustrated. As British writer Samuel Butler was quoted as saying in the nineteenth century: "Life is like giving a concert on the violin while learning to play the instrument." Much more recently, American author Saul Bellow likened it to "concertizing and practicing scales at the same time."

Our feelings may get the better of us, Neil Anderson says, but we are responsible for our thinking and our beliefs. "You are not shaped as much by your environment as you are by your perception of your environment," he wrote in *Victory over the Darkness*. "If what you believe does not reflect truth, then what you feel does not reflect reality. . . . Remember: Your emotions are a product of how you perceived the event, not the event itself."[7]

What if you chose to perceive your joblessness as an opportunity for character building? Child psychologists talk about maturity in terms of "frustration tolerance" in everyday life. When I measure myself by that gauge, I shudder. Ornithologists tell of the value of struggle in the birth of a bird. If the egg is punctured to "help" along the process, the hatchling is less likely to survive, failing to develop the requisite strength through the struggle of the birth process. The suggestion is not just that adversity and struggle are a normal part of life, but that they may be *essential* to life. I recognize that this is not a popular view today, but I believe it's an important perspective for those wounded in the economic theater.

Speaker and author Tim Hansel described this perspective well in his book, *You Gotta Keep Dancin':*

> The big dream in our society is that if we work hard
> enough, we will eventually be able to experience a life with-

out limitations or difficulties. It is also one of the biggest sources of friction in our society, creating disappointment, unnecessary suffering, and missed opportunities to live a full life. Some people spend their entire life waiting for that which will never, and can never, happen. . . .

One of the greatest tragedies of our modern civilization is that you and I can live a trivial life and get away with it. One of the great advantages of pain and suffering is that it forces us to break through our superficial crusts to discover life on a deeper and more meaningful level. . . . Another advantage of disadvantages is that we have the opportunity to be transformed by our suffering.[8]

Here is a question worth pondering: When it comes right down to it, is there any such thing as true earthly security? I think not. And I believe the reason is to turn our hearts toward eternal things. To quote the world's greatest Teacher:

Do not store up for yourselves treasures on earth, where moth and rust destroy, and where thieves break in and steal. But store up for yourselves treasures in heaven, where moth and rust do not destroy, and where thieves do not break in and steal. For where your treasure is, there your heart will be also. (Matthew 6:19–21)

What are treasures in heaven? In work/life terms, I would suggest they include Bolles's triad of finding God, making the world a better place, and exercising your gift in your life mission. I would also suggest they specifically do not include the accumulation of personal possessions and investing oneself in the climbing of career ladders, especially to the exclusion of family and other human relationships.

Bolles has written eloquently about depression and its emotional and spiritual sources—stored-up anger and a sense of abandonment. There's also a mental source, he says—meaninglessness. In *The Three Boxes of Life*, he tells of a study of surgical patients who found meaning to be the single biggest factor in successful post-operative recovery.

> The more the patient believed that there was no such thing as a meaningless experience, the faster the patient healed. Thus, spiritual survival seems to require that there be some meaning to everything that happens, even if that meaning is not evident to us at the time that we are going through the experience.[9]

I am suggesting that in our adversity this meaning is best found in the context of our personal, earthly mission and in our ultimate, eternal mission. In *Redeemed Ambition*, Ralph Mattson wrote: "If you want to know my will, you will have to come into personal contact with me. If you want to know God's will, you will have to come into personal contact with Him."[10] This may be that opportunity. Don't let it pass you by.

NEW BEGINNINGS

Finally, the most encouraging message I can think of to leave with all job prospectors and others seeking to reinvent their careers is another sign on the wall at the Cuyahoga County Reemployment Services Center:

> *The lowest ebb is the turn of the tide.*
> —Henry Wadsworth Longfellow

In a world of sea changes, may this be the turn of *your* tide.

☞ Use this time in your life not just to reinvent your career, but to reinvent yourself mentally, emotionally, and spiritually. If you do that, it will have been worth it all.

NOTES

1. David M. Noer, *Healing the Wounds: Overcoming the Trauma of Lay-offs and Revitalizing Downsized Organizations* (San Francisco: Jossey-Bass, 1993), 153.
2. Richard Nelson Bolles, *The 1996 What Color Is Your Parachute?* (Berkeley, Calif.: Ten Speed Press, 1996), 449.
3. Ibid., 458.
4. Ralph T. Mattson, *Redeemed Ambition: Balancing the Drive to Succeed in Your Work* (Chicago: Moody, 1995), 110.
5. Dan B. Allender and Tremper Longman III, *Bold Love: The Courageous Practice of Life's Ultimate Influence* (Colorado Springs, Colo.: NavPress, 1992), 63.
6. Bolles, *What Color Is Your Parachute?* 95.
7. Neil T. Anderson, *Victory over the Darkness: Realizing the Power of Your Identity in Christ* (Ventura, Calif.: Regal, 1990), 179–80, 199.
8. Tim Hansel, *You Gotta Keep Dancin'* (Elgin, Ill.: David C. Cook, 1985), 94–96.
9. Richard Nelson Bolles, *The Three Boxes of Life: And How to Get Out of Them* (Berkeley, Calif.: Ten Speed Press, 1978, 1981), 354.
10. Mattson, *Redeemed Ambition,* 109.

APPENDIX: RESOURCES

I n keeping with our principle of core competencies, I hope *Reinventing Your Career* proves
to be the best book pound-for-pound in its
particular niche—re-creating your work/life in
terms of meaning, purpose, and mission. But it is by no
means intended to be the final word on all subjects related to
unemployment, careers, and job prospecting. In fact, my
research has impressed me with the great wealth of excellent
material and resources that is already available. There are
entire books, for example, devoted just to the subject of résumé writing. This chapter is an attempt to highlight some of
those wide-ranging resources. Again, it is by no means
exhaustive, but it's a reasonable start.

For sheer comprehensiveness, insight, and thoroughness, nothing can surpass Richard N. Bolles's *What
Color Is Your Parachute?* This is the resource you would
take to the desert island if you had to choose just one career
book—and assuming they were taking applications at the
coconut grove. It has been updated and reissued annually

for a quarter of a century and is available in foreign editions, including Italian, Polish, Spanish, French, Dutch, and Japanese. It is the standard by which all others are to be measured and is a perfect ten in user-friendliness and presentation. With its clear, conversational tone and copious graphics and old-time cartoons and illustrations, *What Color Is Your Parachute?* is a sheer delight.

It is a hefty softcover—"trade paper"—at 480 pages, published by Ten Speed Press in Berkeley, California, at $14.95. It is such a large book that I have never read it from cover to cover, but it's one of those books that sucks me in for fifteen or twenty minutes at a time at whatever section I happen to open it. It is so complete in its approach to everything—from job hunting methods to the job interview and salary negotiations—that it could almost be used in place of a live human career counselor. But if you're looking for one of those, you can find them listed by state in "The Pink Pages," a hundred-page appendix of resources, including even computer software.

THE VIRTUAL JOB SEARCH

Speaking of computers, is the Internet a good job-hunting vehicle? An incredibly short time ago, the answer would have been "forget it," unless you're a techie. When I was newly out of work—spring of 1995—jobs posted on online services were largely limited to computer-related positions and other technical-type jobs with maybe a smattering of sales. Only a year later, it's an entirely different picture.

"The Internet is a fabulous resource for job seekers," said Ri Regina, our ex-NCR employee turned Web site entrepreneur. "There's an incredible wealth of information out there. Almost every major employer has jobs listed as part of its Web site."

And in the future, she predicts, the Net will become the preferred avenue for job prospecting. The credit information service Dunn & Bradstreet provides an online employment resource that can be searched by entering occupational parameters. The same thing can be done on the Web using a search engine such as Yahoo, InfoSeek, AltaVista, or Excite!, said Ri. Search parameters should include terms such as "job opportunity," "career," "human resources," "new position," and your occupational category, such as "public relations" or "graphic design."

To search via Excite!, for example, which is a natural language (laymens' terms) search engine, enter: *http://www.excite.com*. Electronic job prospecting services such as E-Span are also available through the major online services, such as America Online. (Adams Business Communications and Work/Life, Inc., can be e-mailed through AOL at Stephen36@aol.com. By the time you read this, I expect to have my own home page on the Web.) Another popular job service on the Web is the Online Career Center: *http://www.occ.com/occ*. Or do you want to be able to access tens of thousands of help-wanted ads from six major metropolitan American cities electronically? Then try Careerpath at: *http://www.careerpath.com*.

Some predict that in the not-too-distant future employers and job prospectors will be so attuned to the virtual job search that even the job interview itself will be conducted online in a "chat" session. According to an article by the *New York Times* News Service, which participates in Careerpath, the electronic job prospector enjoys the advantage in prospective employers' eyes of being regarded as technically savvy. But a couple of cautions: Until the virtual job search does become *the* preferred method of prospecting, it will continue to be the province of Fortune 500 type of organizations, while career counselors typically advise prospects to improve their odds by applying to the smaller companies. Also, remember that the Internet is national and international. If you're committed to staying in Abilene or Altoona or Anchorage, it's overkill.

LIBRARIES

Libraries, too, are getting into the information technology act in the form of online services, databases, and CD-ROM. One such resource is American Business Disc, a database of U.S. businesses searchable by Standard Industrial Classification (SIC) codes. Another is called OASYS. Learning the four-digit SIC code for your occupational area can be a useful research tool in identifying potential employers. The code can be found in a publication called the *Standard Industrial Classification Manual*. Libraries also maintain periodicals like the *National Business Employment Weekly*, and some even subscribe to such things as national job listings on microfiche that are updated weekly.

Another useful resource is described by Annette L. Segall in her book *Beyond Blue Suits and Résumés:*

> Business InfoTrac is a terrific online system that contains information on 100,000 U.S. corporations, mostly privately held. You don't have to be a computer whiz to use this and, of course, you can always ask the librarian for help. Just type in the name of the company you're researching and you can get key facts about the organization as well as recent articles about the company. Abstracts or entire texts of those articles are available through Business InfoTrac.

Beyond Blue Suits and Resumes, subtitled *Proven Methods Insure Your Job-Finding Success*, is one of the most practical job-prospecting books on the market with helpful sections such as goal setting, networking, and interviewing. It is a 239-page, $14.95 trade paperback, written by a career management consultant and published in 1995 by York Publishing Company. If it is not available at your library or bookstore, it can be ordered through the mail by writing Segall's business, Step to Success, P.O. Box 18432, Cleveland, Ohio, 44118-0432.

Another useful book from a somewhat different perspective is *Surviving Unemployment: A Family Handbook for Weathering Hard Times,* by Cathy Beyer, Doris Pike, and Loretta McGovern—a 296-page trade paperback published by Henry Holt at $10.95. I particularly like its practical tips, such as how to cut expenses during layoff time, budget work sheets, and suggested letters that can be written to creditors, utilities, mortgage companies, and landlords asking for a deferred payment schedule. I also like Cliff Hakim's books *When You Lose Your Job* and *We Are All Self-Employed,* which I have referred to in earlier chapters, for their great utility and insight.

A standard reference published by the federal government is the *Dictionary of Occupational Titles (DOT),* which lists thousands of vocations systematically using a nine-digit occupational code. Description for a goat herder: "Attends herd of goats: Herds goats from corral to fresh pastures. Assists does during kidding season." And that's no joke. It's a 411.687-014. The first three digits identify the eighty-three career divisions and groupings among the nine major occupational clusters, in this case agricultural, fishery, forestry, and related. (The other eight are professional, technical, and managerial; clerical and sales; service; processing; machine trades; benchwork; structural; and miscellaneous.)

The middle three digits identify "worker function" requirements of a job in relation to data, people, and things. The higher the number, the less cerebral and closer to manual labor. The goat herder's 687, for example, translates into comparing (data), taking instructions/helping (people), and handling (things)—the highest number in each category. The last three digits differentiate a particular occupation from all others.

Another example: The *DOT* defines a keyliner as one who "assembles typeset copy and artwork into pasteup for printing reproduction; measures and marks board according to graphic designer or artist's layout." Its *DOT* number is 972.381-030. The middle 381 translates into compiling (data), taking instructions/helping (people), and precision working (things). *DOT* numbering is the standard classification system used in most occupational references.

One such standard reference is the *Occupational Outlook Handbook*, published by the U.S. Department of Labor Bureau of Labor Statistics. It contains more descriptive information in layman's terms in areas such as job-specific employment outlooks, the nature of the work, working conditions, earnings, and qualifications. Other helpful references include the *Guide for Occupational Exploration* and the *Dictionary of Holland Occupational Codes*, among others. Ask your reference or business librarian for assistance.

THE SOURCEBOOK

In this information age, libraries are really diversifying their services to the public. The county library system where I live even provides a career guidance and job search assistance center at one of its regional branches, called InfoPLACE, with trained professional counselors to help job prospectors. They also publish a very useful resource of their own called *Career Vision: The Sourcebook*, a sixty-nine-page guidebook that addresses steps in making a career decision, tackling a job search, how to obtain government jobs, and help with relocation.

The Sourcebook explains how to develop a self-marketing strategy through the use of want ads, employment agencies and temporary help firms, direct contact with targeted organizations, and contacts/networking. Some of its information is specific to Ohio, but most of it is applicable anywhere. It also gives useful synopses of other helpful resources and references. For example, if you are interested in career planning from the perspective of personality preferences and types, such as the Myers-Briggs inventory, it provides information on nine such books. One example:

Type Talk: Or How to Determine Your Personality Type

and Change Your Life. Otto Kroeger and Janet M. Thuesen. New York: Delacorte, 1988. 155.264-K913t

This introduction to the role of personality preferences revealed by the Myers-Briggs Type Indicator describes in fascinating and amusing detail the sixteen personality types and how they operate in such areas as marriage, parenthood, work, and career selection.

Here are some synopses of good general job search books, according to *The Sourcebook* (used by permission of the Cuyahoga County Public Library):

The Complete Job Search Handbook: All the Skills You Need to Get Any Job and Have a Good Time Doing It. Howard E. Figler. New York: Holt, 1988. Revised and expanded edition. 650.14-F468c2

A "classic" career planning and job search guide, this book by a top expert is designed to serve as either a quick resource for specific concerns (many chapters are self-contained) or as a comprehensive A-to-Z manual. Includes tips on improving communicating and assertiveness skills and a section on "Special Problems and Solutions." One of the few books that describes different types of informational interviews.

Super Job Search: The Complete Manual for Job-Seekers and Career-Changers. Peter K. Studner. Los Angeles: Jamenair, 1991. 650.14-St94s4

This title lives up to its name as a comprehensive, right-on-target job search book. It includes financial matters during job searches, job search organization, goal setting, assessing and describing accomplishments, résumé writing, creating a marketing plan, networking, and telemarketing, plus arranging and handling three kinds of interviews: (1) the research or information interview, (2) the advice interview, and (3) the direct (employment) interview. Sample cover letters and résumés are included.

Guerrilla Tactics in the New Job Market. Tom Jackson. New York: Bantam, 1991. Second edition. 650.14J 138g2

A tell-it-like-it-is guide to the swiftly changing, highly competitive job market, this readable job search book helps you maneuver through the employment maze with the assistance of seventy-seven specific tactics.

Job Hunting After 50: Strategies for Success. Samuel N. Ray. New York: Wiley, 1991. 650.140844-R213j

Geared toward older workers who have taken early retirement, have been laid off, or are looking for new challenges, this informative and practical job-hunting guide addresses such issues as overcoming age discrimination, handling age issues in the interview, and finding employers who value experience over youth.

The Overnight Job Change Strategy. Donald Asher. Berkeley, Calif.: Ten Speed, 1993. 650.14-As35oj

A point-by-point fresh and realistic approach to targeting, researching, and approaching employers with a finely honed message detailing exactly why they should hire *you*.

Résumés Don't Get Jobs: The Realities and Myths of Job Hunting. Bob Weinstein. New York: McGraw-Hill, 1993. 650.14-W433r

This gritty, no-holds-barred guide to job hunting in tough economic times effectively outlines real-world strategies while deflating job search mythologies.

Sharkproof: Get the Job You Want, Keep the Job You Love . . . in Today's Frenzied Job Market. Harvey B. Mackay. New York: HarperBusiness, 1993. 650.14-M192s

 A colorful, feisty book by a CEO on finding and keeping jobs in a tough employment market. Liberal use of anecdotes to illustrate his points.

The Women's Job Search Handbook: With Issues and Insights into the Workplace. Gerri B. Bloomberg and Margaret Hodge Holden. Charlotte, Vt.: Williamson, 1991. 650.14082-B623w

 A classic job search text with useful skill exercises, psychological focusing, networking, and explicit search strategies. For women and men of all ages.

A Big Splash in a Small Pond: Finding a Great Job in a Small Company. R. Linda Resnick with Kerry H. Pechter. New York: Simon & Schuster, 1994. 650.14-R312b

 In the turbulent American job market, with waves of corporate downsizing, the job growth is in small companies. A "must read" for anyone interested in understanding, locating, and getting hired by small companies. Also helps you determine if you have the right stuff for working in a small business.

 As you can see, *Career Vision: The Sourcebook* can shortcut a lot of research for you. It can be ordered by mail for $9.99 (includes shipping and handling) from Public Relations Division, Cuyahoga County Public Library, 2111 Snow Road, Parma, Ohio, 44134-2792. Make checks payable to Cuyahoga County Public Library.

ASSESSMENT / INVENTORIES

As mentioned earlier in this book, taking an inventory of your values, skills, abilities, and preferences is invaluable to getting your bearings and reinventing your career. Most instruments used in that kind of assessment are designed to be administered and evaluated by professionals, such as a career counselor. There are some, however, that can be self-administered. If you are not already planning to use the services of a career counselor or a job placement service, you may want to avail yourself of such an opportunity.

One such instrument is the Self-Directed Search (SDS) Specimen Set, which can be obtained from Psychological Assessment Resources, Inc., Box 998, Odessa, Florida, 33556. Another excellent resource is "Career Pathways," with which I have some personal experience. (My son took it before going to college.) It is distributed by Christian Financial Concepts, Inc. (CFC), an organization devoted to helping families live debt-free, founded by well-known financial counselor Larry Burkett.

CFC's description:

> The *Career Pathways Full Assessment Package* is a testing assessment program that provides valuable insights about one's personality, interests, skills, and work priorities. This mail-order assessment is an important first step in the process of finding direction for your career search and will help you learn more about your unique pattern and the types of occupations which match it.

In my son's case, it confirmed that a pre-seminary program that interested him would be a good choice.

This assessment can be ordered by writing Career Pathways, P.O. Box 1476, Gainesville, Georgia, 30503-1476, or by calling 1-800-722-1976. Other resources available through Career Pathways include the books *Your Career in Changing Times* and *Finding the Career That Fits You*, a Career Exploration Kit (for students in grades eight to ten), and a forty-page Personality Analysis. For information on other helpful materials, particularly in the area of family budgeting and planning, write Christian Financial Concepts, Inc., P.O. Box 2377, Gainesville, Georgia, 30503-2377. I particularly like a seventy-nine page booklet by Lee Ellis called *Job Search Strategies* for the amount of useful, step-by-step information condensed into a small package that's a quick read.

MISCELLANEOUS

In the don't-overlook-the-obvious department: Your local bureau of employment services or unemployment office may provide job placement services or counseling in addition to basic unemployment benefits. Services vary from state to state, and sometimes they are not well promoted or advertised. Ask. Another major source of assistance: Programs funded through the federal Job Training Partnership Act (JTPA) provide retraining and relocation services. Many of the participants in the Cuyahoga County Reemployment Services Center described earlier have received valuable training and education benefits through the JTPA. There is a qualifying process.

For further information, according to *Surviving Unemployment:* Look for a JTPA office in your area or inquire through your local unemployment or job service office. JTPA is administered by the Employment and Training Administration of the U.S. Department of Labor, 200 Constitution Ave., N.W., Washington, D.C., 20210. Call its office of Public Affairs at 202-219-6871 for more information.

Suppose you don't get another job, but you pursue self-employment. How do you price your services? Here's one formula for calculating a billable hourly rate, which I have adapted from several sources:

> Work backward. Say an in-house staffer would be paid $45,000 a year for the same work in your locale. That's the market rate. Divide by 1,500, which is the number of billable hours you might reasonably expect in a year (thirty hours a week times fifty weeks), considering client development, marketing, and other nonbillable time, yielding a base of $30 an hour. In all cases, adapt this to your personal situation. If, for example, you really are billing out forty hours a week, your annual hourly factor would be 2,000 (forty hours a week times fifty weeks).
>
> Then add another 33 percent to cover the cost of taxes and fringe benefits that you bear (for example, Social Security, health insurance, and retirement) plus another factor for your own costs of doing business (overhead, such as rent, equipment, supplies). Some accountants use a 35 percent factor for fringe costs. The overhead cost factor will vary much more, depending on the nature of your business. If you're a writer, like me, you may not have much more than the costs of a personal computer, paper, long-distance phone calls, and the like. Check with an accountant for guidance.

In our hypothetical case, those three calculations would look like this:

> $30 (base rate) + $10 (33 percent fringes) + $6 (20 percent overhead) = $46 per hour.

Therefore, you know you would be charging a fair rate somewhere around $45 to $50 an hour. With a little research you also may be able to obtain suggested flat fee schedules from professional organizations and publications. That gives you the flexibility to bid a job two different ways. If you're really hungry, the flat fee is more likely to win the job because your prospective client knows his expense is capped. The downside for you is that things generally take longer than projected, and you may end up eating those costs.

If you are interested in information
about other books written from a
biblical perspective, please write
to the following address:

Northfield Publishing
215 West Locust Street
Chicago, IL 60610